DAILY DEVOTIONAL FOR
Hardworking Moms

5-MINUTE GOD'S PROMISES DAILY DEVOTIONAL FOR HARDWORKING MOMS

ANCHORED GRACE PUBLISHING

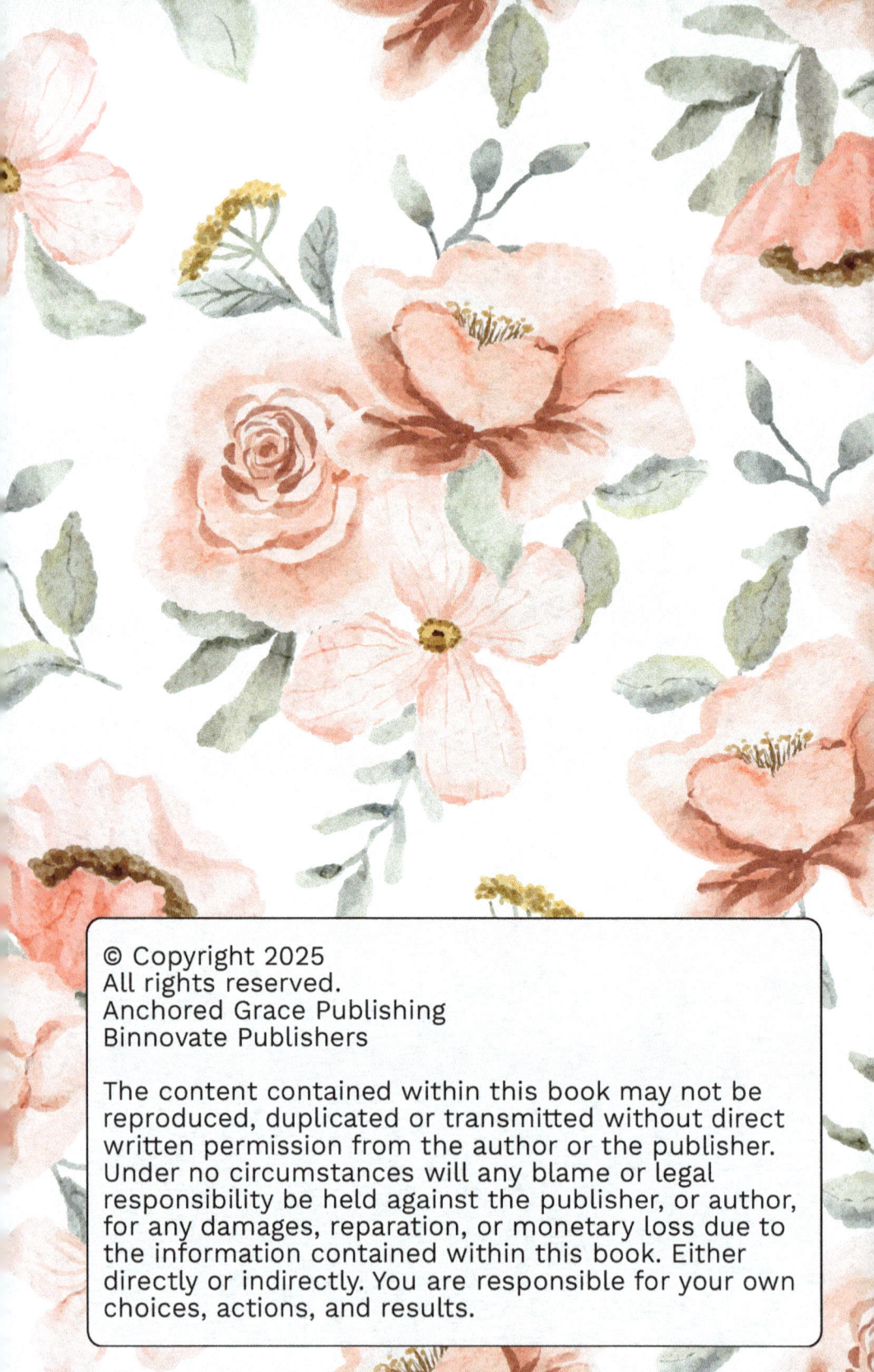

A Gift for You

Thank you for choosing this devotional.

To support your journey of faith, we created a special gift bundle for our readers.

Inside the Anchored Grace Reader Gift Bundle, you will receive:

- A free digital devotional

- Printable prayer journal pages

- Scripture reflection cards

- Bonus devotionals for different seasons of life

- Daily encouragement from Anchored Grace

Simply scan the QR code below or visit the link to receive your free bundle.

devo.anchoredgraces.com/workingmomsgift

Scan the QR code with your phone camera or type the link into your browser.

We pray these resources continue to encourage your heart each day.

NEW BEGINNINGS WITH GOD

"Forget the former things; do not dwell on the past.
See, I am doing a new thing!" **Isaiah 43:18-19**

DEVOTIONAL

Embrace the promise of Isaiah 43:18-19 as a beautiful invitation to release the past and welcome new beginnings. God lovingly calls us to let go of old hurt and disappointment, urging us to see the fresh paths He is creating. Reflect on the blessings ahead and the transformation waiting for you. Each day is an opportunity to step into His light, nurturing your spirit and deepening your faith. Trust that in your new journey, God is always with you.

DAILY REFLECTION

In what ways can you actively embrace the promise of new beginnings in your life, letting go of past hurts and disappointments, and how might you open yourself to the blessings and transformations that lie ahead?

PRAYER

Gracious God, help me to release the burdens of my past and to embrace the promise of new beginnings, trusting that You are faithfully guiding me toward fresh paths filled with hope and transformation. May I open my heart to the blessings that await and nurture my spirit as I step into the light of Your love, knowing that with each new day, You walk beside me.

TRUSTING GOD'S TIMING

"But those who hope in the Lord will renew their strength. They will soar on wings like eagles; they will run and not grow weary, they will walk and not be faint." **Isaiah 40:31**

DEVOTIONAL

In the hustle of life, it's easy to question God's timing. Yet Isaiah 40:31 reminds us that hope in the Lord renews our strength. Trusting His timing can transform weariness into wings, allowing us to rise above our struggles. When we surrender our schedules to Him, we find peace and purpose instead of frustration. Embrace the journey, knowing that with each step of faith, God is crafting a beautiful story in your life. Let patience cultivate your heart.

DAILY REFLECTION

In the midst of your busy life, how can you practice surrendering your schedule to God and embrace His timing, allowing His hope to renew your strength and transform your journey?

PRAYER

Dear Lord, in the midst of life's busyness, help me to release my tight grip on my plans and trust in Your perfect timing. Grant me the patience to embrace each moment, knowing that with You guiding my path, my weariness can be transformed into renewed strength and purpose.

EMBRACING GRACE, NOT PERFECTION

"My grace is sufficient for you, for my power is made perfect in weakness." **2 Corinthians 12:9**

DEVOTIONAL

In a world that often demands perfection, remember that God's grace is your refuge. 2 Corinthians 12:9 reminds us that His power shines brightest in our weaknesses. Instead of striving for an unattainable ideal, embrace the grace offered to you. Each flaw tells a story of growth and reliance on Him. Allow your imperfections to draw you closer to God, revealing His strength in your journey. Today, rest in His sufficiency and find beauty in your authentic self.

DAILY REFLECTION

As you consider the message of God's grace in your life, how can you intentionally embrace your imperfections as opportunities for growth and deeper reliance on Him, rather than striving for perfection? Reflect on a specific area where you have felt pressure to be flawless, and think about how you can shift your perspective to celebrate your authenticity and God's strength in that space.

PRAYER

Dear God, in a world that often seeks perfection, help me to embrace the grace that you freely offer, recognizing that my imperfections are not a burden but a pathway to deeper growth and reliance on you. May I find beauty in my authentic self, trusting that your strength shines through my struggles, and celebrate each flaw as a testament to your unwavering love and guidance in my life.

FINDING PEACE IN GOD'S PRESENCE

"Peace I leave with you; my peace I give to you." **John 14:27**

DEVOTIONAL

When we feel worried or scared, it's important to remember that Jesus gives us peace. In John 14:27, He says, "Peace I leave with you; my peace I give to you." This means that even on tough days, we can find calmness in God's presence. Take a moment to talk to God and ask for His peace. Trust that He is with you, guiding you, and helping you feel safe. Finding peace with God is always possible.

DAILY REFLECTION

Reflect on a time when you felt worried or scared. How did you seek peace in that moment, and what do you think it means to trust in God's presence to help you feel safe? Take a moment to pray and ask for His peace in your life right now.

PRAYER

Dear Jesus, thank you for your promise of peace when we feel worried or scared. Help me to remember that you are always with me, guiding me and filling my heart with calmness, no matter what I face.

YOUR IDENTITY IN CHRIST

"Therefore, if anyone is in Christ, he is a new creation; the old has passed away, behold, the new has come." **2 Corinthians 5:17**

When we believe in Jesus, we become new! This is what 2 Corinthians 5:17 tells us. Our old mistakes and worries are gone, and God sees us in a fresh way. Imagine a caterpillar turning into a butterfly—beautiful and free! Every day, we can choose to live in this new life, filled with love, hope, and purpose. Remember, you are special and loved by God. Let His Spirit guide you in becoming the person you were meant to be.

Think about a time when you felt overlooked or not appreciated. How can remembering that God sees you as new and special help you change how you feel about that situation? What is one way you can choose to live in that new life today?

Dear God, thank you for making us new and seeing us as special, just like a beautiful butterfly. Help us remember your love and choose to live each day with hope and purpose, knowing we are always cherished by you.

GOD'S FAITHFULNESS THROUGH THE YEARS

"Great is your faithfulness." **Lamentations 3:23**

DEVOTIONAL

God's faithfulness is like a warm blanket on a chilly night, always there to comfort us. In Lamentations 3:23, we learn that His faithfulness is great—it never changes, no matter what happens in our lives. Each day is a new opportunity to see how God cares for us. When things are hard or confusing, remember that God is with you, holding your hand through every season. Trust in His promises, for He will always be by your side.

DAILY REFLECTION

How can you remember and share moments in your life when you felt God's comforting presence, like a warm blanket, during challenging times?

PRAYER

Dear God, thank you for being our warm blanket of comfort, always wrapping us in Your love and faithfulness, no matter what we face. Help us to remember and share the times when we felt Your gentle presence, guiding us through life's challenges with Your sweet embrace.

YOUR IDENTITY IN CHRIST

"Therefore, if anyone is in Christ, he is a new creation; the old has passed away, behold, the new has come." **2 Corinthians 5:17**

DEVOTIONAL

When we believe in Jesus, we become new! This is what 2 Corinthians 5:17 tells us. Our old mistakes and worries are gone, and God sees us in a fresh way. Imagine a caterpillar turning into a butterfly—beautiful and free! Every day, we can choose to live in this new life, filled with love, hope, and purpose. Remember, you are special and loved by God. Let His Spirit guide you in becoming the person you were meant to be.

DAILY REFLECTION

Think about a time when you felt overlooked or not appreciated. How can remembering that God sees you as new and special help you change how you feel about that situation? What is one way you can choose to live in that new life today?

PRAYER

Dear God, thank you for making us new and seeing us as special, just like a beautiful butterfly. Help us remember your love and choose to live each day with hope and purpose, knowing we are always cherished by you.

GOD'S FAITHFULNESS THROUGH THE YEARS

"Great is your faithfulness." **Lamentations 3:23**

DEVOTIONAL

God's faithfulness is like a warm blanket on a chilly night, always there to comfort us. In Lamentations 3:23, we learn that His faithfulness is great—it never changes, no matter what happens in our lives. Each day is a new opportunity to see how God cares for us. When things are hard or confusing, remember that God is with you, holding your hand through every season. Trust in His promises, for He will always be by your side.

DAILY REFLECTION

How can you remember and share moments in your life when you felt God's comforting presence, like a warm blanket, during challenging times?

PRAYER

Dear God, thank you for being our warm blanket of comfort, always wrapping us in Your love and faithfulness, no matter what we face. Help us to remember and share the times when we felt Your gentle presence, guiding us through life's challenges with Your sweet embrace.

One Week Together

You've just completed your first week of devotionals.

If these reflections have brought peace or encouragement into your day, would you consider sharing a short Amazon review?

devo.anchoredgraces.com/workingmoms

Your words help other women discover devotionals that may support them on their own faith journey.

Thank you for spending these moments in reflection.

COURAGE TO LET GO

"Cast all your anxiety on him because he cares for you."
1 Peter 5:7

DEVOTIONAL

Sometimes we carry heavy worries that weigh us down, like a big backpack full of rocks. But 1 Peter 5:7 reminds us that we can give our worries to God because He cares for us. Imagine your worries floating away like balloons! When we let go of what troubles us, we make space for joy and peace. This week, let's practice casting our anxieties to God. Trust that He is there to hold you up and help you grow.

DAILY REFLECTION

What are some worries you can let go of this week, and how do you think it will feel to release them to God?

PRAYER

Dear God, help us as we learn to let go of our worries and give them to You, knowing that You care for us deeply. May we feel the lightness in our hearts as we trust in Your love, making room for joy and peace in our lives.

WHEN YOU FEEL OVERLOOKED

"But the Lord said to Samuel, 'Do not consider his appearance or his height, for I have rejected him. The Lord does not look at the things people look at. People look at the outward appearance, but the Lord looks at the heart.'" **1 Samuel 16:7**

DEVOTIONAL

Sometimes, we feel unnoticed or less important than others. But God sees us differently! In 1 Samuel 16:7, we learn that God looks at our hearts, not our looks or height. This reminds us that what truly matters is who we are inside. When you feel overlooked, remember that God cherishes you and values your kindness, love, and faith. Spend time with Him, and let His love fill your heart. You are special just the way you are.

DAILY REFLECTION

Think about a time when you felt unnoticed or not as important as others. How can remembering that God values your heart and who you are inside help you see your own worth differently? What are some ways you can express kindness and love to yourself and others, even when you might feel overlooked?

PRAYER

Dear God, thank you for seeing the beauty in our hearts and reminding us that we are cherished just as we are. Help us to embrace our unique worth and share kindness and love with ourselves and others, even when we feel overlooked.

RESTING IN HIS PROMISES

"Come to me, all you who are weary and burdened, and I will give you rest." **Matthew 11:28**

DEVOTIONAL

When we feel tired or weighed down by worries, Jesus invites us to come to Him. He knows our struggles and wants to help us find peace. Just like a cozy blanket on a chilly day, His promises wrap us in love and comfort. When we trust Him, we can let go of our burdens and rest. Take a moment today to talk to Jesus. Share your worries, and remember, He is always ready to lift you up.

DAILY REFLECTION

Reflect on a time when you felt overwhelmed by worries. How can you invite Jesus into that situation today? What would it feel like to share your worries with Him and trust in His promise to bring you peace?

PRAYER

Dear Jesus, when my heart feels heavy and my thoughts are full of worries, help me to remember that I can come to You for comfort. Thank You for wrapping me in Your love and peace, so I can share my burdens and trust in Your promises.

BEAUTY FROM BROKENNESS

"He heals the brokenhearted and binds up their wounds." **Psalm 147:3**

DEVOTIONAL

Sometimes, life can feel tough and sad, like when we get hurt or lose something special. But remember, God is always there to help us heal. Psalm 147:3 tells us that He heals the brokenhearted and binds up their wounds. This means that even when we feel broken, God can turn our pain into something beautiful. When we trust Him and talk to Him, we can find comfort and strength. Let's open our hearts to His love and healing.

DAILY REFLECTION

How have you felt God's love and healing in your life during tough or sad times? Take a moment to think about a time when you felt broken or hurt. What did you do to find comfort and strength, and how can you remember to trust God in those moments?

PRAYER

Dear God, thank You for being with us when we feel sad or hurt, and for helping us heal our broken hearts. Please remind us to trust in Your love and to share our feelings with You, so we can find comfort and strength in every moment.

January 13

THE POWER OF PRAYER

"And whatever you ask in prayer, believing, you will receive." **Matthew 21:22**

DEVOTIONAL

Prayer is a special way to talk to God. When we pray, we share our hopes, worries, and dreams with Him. Matthew 21:22 reminds us that if we truly believe, God hears us and will respond. Think of prayer as a bridge connecting you to God's love and power. Take time every day to pray, whether it's thankfulness for your blessings or asking for help. Trust that God is listening, and He cares about you deeply.

DAILY REFLECTION

How do you feel when you take a moment to share your thoughts and feelings with God through prayer? What are some hopes, worries, or dreams you would like to talk to Him about today?

PRAYER

Dear God, thank you for being my loving friend who listens to my hopes and worries. Help me to remember that every time I pray, I'm sharing my heart with you, and I trust that you are always with me, caring for me deeply.

January 14

JOY IN THE ORDINARY

"This is the day that the Lord has made; let us rejoice and be glad in it." **Psalm 118:24**

DEVOTIONAL

Today is a special gift from God! Each morning, when you wake up, remember that He made this day just for you. No matter how ordinary it may seem—like a sunny sky, a warm meal, or time with friends—these little moments are filled with joy. When we focus on the good around us, we can see God's love shining through. Let's thank Him for today and choose to rejoice in every simple, beautiful moment.

DAILY REFLECTION

Reflect on a moment from today that made you feel thankful. What was happening around you, and how did it show you God's love?

PRAYER

Dear God, thank You for this special gift of today, filled with little moments that remind us of Your love. Help us to see the beauty in our everyday lives and to cherish the joy in our hearts.

THE POWER OF PRAYER

"If any of you lacks wisdom, let him ask of God, who gives to all liberally and without reproach, and it will be given to him." **James 1:5**

DEVOTIONAL

God wants to help us make good choices every day. James 1:5 tells us that if we ask Him for wisdom, He will give it to us generously. Imagine a wise friend who always knows the right thing to say! When we face tough decisions or don't know what to do, we can talk to God and ask for His guidance. Let's remember to pray and listen, trusting that He can help us grow and shine His light.

DAILY REFLECTION

Think about a time when you had to make a tough choice. How did you feel, and what did you do to find the right answer? Can you think of a way to ask God for wisdom next time you face a decision?

PRAYER

Dear God, thank You for always being there to help us make good choices. Please give us wisdom and guide our hearts when we face tough decisions, so we can shine Your light in everything we do.

FREEDOM FROM FEAR

"For God has not given us a spirit of fear, but of power and of love and of a sound mind." **2 Timothy 1:7**

DEVOTIONAL

God wants us to live boldly and happily, not scared or worried. In 2 Timothy 1:7, we learn that He gives us strength, love, and a calm mind. When we feel afraid, we can remember that God is with us, helping us to be brave. Take a deep breath and pray, asking God to replace your fear with His power. Trust that He loves you and is always by your side, guiding you every step of the way.

DAILY REFLECTION

How can you remind yourself of God's presence when you feel scared or worried, and what steps can you take to embrace His strength and love in those moments?

PRAYER

Dear God, thank you for always being with us and giving us strength and love when we feel scared; help us to remember that you calm our hearts and make us brave. Please fill us with your peace, guiding us to live boldly and happily, knowing you are by our side every step of the way.

When we feel scared or worried, we can remind ourselves that God is always with us by taking a moment to breathe deeply and pray, turning our thoughts to His love and strength. Embracing His words and promises can help us feel safe, encouraging us to take small steps forward with faith in our hearts.

A HEART ANCHORED IN HOPE

"May the God of hope fill you with all joy and peace as you trust in Him, so that you may overflow with hope by the power of the Holy Spirit." **Romans 15:13**

DEVOTIONAL

When we trust God, He fills our hearts with joy and peace, even when things seem tough. Imagine hope like sunshine breaking through clouds. As we believe in God and lean on the Holy Spirit, hope shines brighter in us and spills over to others. Remember, every time you feel scared or uncertain, turn to God. He is always ready to fill you with His goodness, helping you stand strong and share His love with everyone around you.

DAILY REFLECTION

How can you remind yourself to trust in God when faced with challenges, and what are some ways you can share the joy and peace you receive from Him with those around you?

PRAYER

Dear God, thank you for being our safe place, filling our hearts with joy and peace, even when things feel wobbly. Help us remember to trust in You and share the hope and love You give us with all our friends and family.

LIVING WITH ETERNAL PURPOSE

"Set your minds on things that are above, not on things that are on earth." **Colossians 3:2**

DEVOTIONAL

What we think about matters! Colossians 3:2 reminds us to focus on what truly lasts—God's love, joy, and kindness. When we set our minds on heavenly things, we see our lives differently. Instead of worrying about little problems, we can share love and help others. Remember, every good deed brings us closer to God. Make time to pray, read the Bible, and share your faith. Each moment spent with God helps us live with eternal purpose.

DAILY REFLECTION

Think about a time when you focused on something small that made you feel worried or upset. How might your feelings change if you shifted your focus to something positive, like helping someone or sharing love? What can you do this week to spend more time on things that bring you closer to God?

PRAYER

Dear God, help us to remember that what we think about matters, and guide us to focus on Your love and the joy of helping others. May we find peace in our hearts as we set our minds on the good and share kindness in our days.

TRUSTING GOD WITH FAMILY

"Commit your way to the Lord; trust in him, and he will act."
Psalm 37:5

DEVOTIONAL

Trusting God with our family is important! In Psalm 37:5, we learn to "commit your way to the Lord; trust in him, and he will act." This means we can share our worries and dreams about our loved ones with God. When we trust Him, He helps us make wise choices and brings peace. Spend a moment today praying for your family, asking God to guide you and them, knowing He loves and cares for each of you.

DAILY REFLECTION

Think about a worry or dream you have for your family. How can you share that with God in prayer today? What kind of peace do you think you might feel when you trust Him with it?

PRAYER

Dear God, we thank You for our family and ask that You help us share our worries and dreams with You. Please guide us, fill our hearts with trust, and bring us peace as we lean on Your love and care.

WHEN YOU NEED STRENGTH

"I can do all things through Christ who strengthens me."
Philippians 4:13

DEVOTIONAL

When you feel weak or unsure, remember Philippians 4:13: "I can do all things through Christ who strengthens me." This means you are never alone! Jesus is always with you, ready to help when things get tough. Whenever you face a challenge, pray and ask for His strength. Trust that with Him by your side, you can overcome anything. As you grow in faith, you'll discover new courage and confidence to face each day with joy!

DAILY REFLECTION

When you think about the challenges you face each day, how can remembering that Jesus is with you strengthen your confidence to tackle them?

PRAYER

Dear Jesus, thank you for being my constant helper and for giving me strength when I feel unsure. Help me remember that with you by my side, I can face any challenge with courage and joy.

LISTENING FOR GOD'S WHISPER

"Be still, and know that I am God." **Psalm 46:10**

DEVOTIONAL

In our busy lives, it's easy to forget to listen for God's voice. Psalm 46:10 invites us to "be still." Imagine finding a quiet place, taking a deep breath, and focusing on God. When we slow down, we can hear His whispers of love, guidance, and comfort. This week, set aside a few moments each day to be still. Trust that God is waiting to speak to you and help you grow closer to Him.

DAILY REFLECTION

As you take a moment to be still this week, how do you feel when you imagine listening for God's whispers? What thoughts or feelings come to mind that you would like to share with Him?

PRAYER

Dear God, help us find moments of stillness in our busy days so we can hear Your whispers of love and guidance. As we sit quietly, may we feel Your presence and share with You our thoughts and feelings, trusting that You are always there to listen.

BECOMING A WOMAN OF THE WORD

"Your word is a lamp to my feet and a light to my path." **Psalm 119:105**

DEVOTIONAL

God's Word is like a flashlight in the dark, guiding us when we feel lost. Psalm 119:105 reminds us that His words help us make good choices and show us the way to live joyfully. Each time we read the Bible, we learn more about God's love and wisdom. Let's spend time with Him daily, inviting His light into our hearts. As we grow closer to God, we become women who shine His light to others.

DAILY REFLECTION

How can you incorporate time spent in God's Word into your daily routine, and in what ways do you believe this will help you shine His light to those around you?

PRAYER

Dear God, thank You for Your Word, which lights our path and helps us see clearly when we feel lost. As we spend time in Your love and wisdom, may our hearts shine brightly with Your light, bringing joy and guidance to everyone around us.

Three Weeks of Reflection

You've now spent several weeks walking through these devotionals.

If this book has encouraged your heart, a brief Amazon review helps other women find the same encouragement.

devo.anchoredgraces.com/workingmoms

Your experience may guide someone else toward the hope they are searching for.

Thank you for being here.

HEALING THROUGH SCRIPTURE

"He heals the brokenhearted and binds up their wounds." **Psalm 147:3**

DEVOTIONAL

When we feel sad or confused, it's comforting to know that God cares deeply for us. The Bible tells us in Psalm 147:3 that "He heals the brokenhearted and binds up their wounds." This means God wants to help us when we're hurting. We can turn to Scripture for comfort and encouragement. When we read His words, we can find peace and strength. Let's remember to pray and ask God to heal our hearts each day.

DAILY REFLECTION

How does knowing that God cares for you when you're feeling sad or confused help you find peace in those moments? Take a moment to think about a time when you felt down and how reading Scripture or praying might have brought you comfort.

PRAYER

Dear God, thank you for always being with us when we feel sad or confused, and for healing our hearts when we are hurting. Help us to remember Your loving words in the Bible, so we can find comfort and strength in You each day.

WHEN LIFE FEELS HEAVY

"Come to me, all you who are weary and burdened, and I will give you rest." **Matthew 11:28**

DEVOTIONAL

When life feels heavy, remember Jesus' invitation: "Come to me, all you who are weary and burdened, and I will give you rest." God wants to carry your worries! Picture Him as a loving friend, ready to help you with your struggles. Take a moment each day to talk to Him, share your burdens, and listen in silence. You'll find comfort in His presence. Trust that He cares for you and will give you peace.

DAILY REFLECTION

Reflect on a time when you felt overwhelmed or burdened. How did you respond to those feelings? Take a moment to consider how inviting Jesus into that situation could have changed your experience. What specific worries can you share with Him today, and how might you feel if you truly trusted that He is ready to help you carry those burdens?

PRAYER

Dear God, when my heart feels heavy and my worries seem too much to carry, I remember that You are always there, ready to help me. I come to You now, sharing my burdens, and I trust in Your loving presence to bring me peace and comfort.

GOD'S GRACE FOR PAST MISTAKES

"But he gives us more grace." **James 4:6**

DEVOTIONAL

Life can be tough, and sometimes we make mistakes. But remember, God loves you no matter what! In James 4:6, we learn that "He gives us more grace." This means that when we mess up, God is there to forgive and help us start fresh. Instead of feeling guilty, we can choose to learn and grow from our errors. Trust in His grace, and let it guide you into becoming a better person every day.

DAILY REFLECTION

Reflect on a time when you made a mistake. How did you feel in that moment, and how can remembering God's grace help you turn that experience into an opportunity for growth?

PRAYER

Dear God, thank you for loving us even when we make mistakes, and for giving us your grace to help us grow and learn each day. Help us to remember that every misstep is a chance to start fresh and become better, knowing you are always by our side.

LIVING LOVED

"We love because he first loved us." **1 John 4:19**

DEVOTIONAL

God's love is like a warm hug that never ends! 1 John 4:19 reminds us that we love others because God loved us first. Every time we show kindness or share a smile, we are sharing His love. Take a moment each day to remember how special you are to God. Let His love fill your heart, and then let it flow out to everyone around you. Living loved means spreading that love every day!

DAILY REFLECTION

How can you show God's love to someone today through a kind act or a smile? Take a moment to think about what that might look like and how it could make both of you feel special.

PRAYER

Dear God, thank you for your never-ending love that warms our hearts like a big, cozy hug. Help us to share that love with others through our kindness and smiles, reminding everyone how special they are, just like we are to you.

DECLUTTERING THE SOUL

"Create in me a clean heart, O God, and renew a right spirit within me." **Psalm 51:10**

DEVOTIONAL

When we feel cluttered inside, it can be hard to see what truly matters. Psalm 51:10 reminds us to ask God to create a clean heart in us. Just like we clean our messy rooms, God helps us clear away our worries, anger, and unkind thoughts. Take a moment to pray and ask Him to renew your spirit. As you let go of what weighs you down, you'll find peace and joy in His love and presence.

DAILY REFLECTION

What are some worries or unkind thoughts that have been cluttering your heart lately, and how can you invite God to help you let go of them so you can feel His peace and joy?

PRAYER

Dear God, please help me to clear away all the worries and unkind thoughts that clutter my heart, and create in me a clean and joyful spirit. I invite Your love to fill me up, so I can let go of what weighs me down and find peace in Your presence.

ROOTED AND GROUNDED IN LOVE

"So that Christ may dwell in your hearts through faith—that you, being rooted and grounded in love." **Ephesians 3:17**

DEVOTIONAL

Today, think about how strong trees grow. Just like trees need deep roots to stand tall and weather storms, we need to be rooted in love. When Christ lives in our hearts, His love helps us grow strong in faith. This love helps us show kindness, patience, and understanding to others. Remember to spend time with God each day, so His love can fill you up and help you share that love with the world around you.

DAILY REFLECTION

Think about a time when you felt loved and strong, like a tree with deep roots. How can you share that love with someone today?

PRAYER

Dear God, thank you for the strong love you give us, like deep roots that help us stand tall and face life's challenges. Please fill our hearts with your love today, so we can share kindness and understanding with everyone around us.

GUARDING YOUR HEART

"Above all else, guard your heart, for everything you do flows from it." **Proverbs 4:23**

DEVOTIONAL

Guarding your heart means protecting your feelings, thoughts, and choices. In Proverbs 4:23, we learn that our hearts are the source of our actions. When we fill our hearts with love, kindness, and God's Word, we make better choices. Spend time with God each day through prayer and reading the Bible. Let His truth shape your heart. Remember, when you guard your heart, you shine His light to others, showing them the beauty of His love.

DAILY REFLECTION

How can you fill your heart with love and kindness today, and what steps will you take to guard it from negative influences?

PRAYER

Dear God, please help me to fill my heart with love and kindness so I can shine your light to those around me. Guide me to make good choices and protect my feelings and thoughts, keeping me close to your truth and love today.

A FAITH THAT ENDURES

"But the one who endures to the end will be saved." **Matthew 24:13**

DEVOTIONAL

Life can be tough, and sometimes we feel like giving up. But Jesus reminds us that those who keep believing and trusting Him until the end will find true joy and salvation. Just like a runner who pushes through the finish line, we must persevere in our faith. When challenges come, remember that God is with you, helping you grow stronger. Keep praying, keep reading the Bible, and trust that your endurance will lead to wonderful blessings.

DAILY REFLECTION

Reflect on a time when you faced a challenge and felt like giving up. How did you manage to keep going, and what role did your faith play in helping you persevere?

PRAYER

Dear Jesus, when life feels heavy and we want to give up, help us to remember that You are always beside us, giving us strength to keep going. May our hearts hold Your promise of joy and salvation, guiding us to trust in Your loving presence through every challenge we face.

STEPPING INTO THE NEW WITH BOLDNESS

"Be strong and courageous; do not be afraid, do not be discouraged, for the Lord your God will be with you wherever you go." **Joshua 1:9**

DEVOTIONAL

Stepping into the new can feel scary, but God is always with us! Just like He told Joshua, we can be strong and brave. When we face changes or challenges, remember that God walks beside us, giving us courage. Each day is an opportunity to trust Him more. Instead of being afraid, let's choose to follow where God leads. Take a deep breath, step forward with confidence, and know that His love surrounds you wherever you go!

DAILY REFLECTION

As you think about the changes you might be facing, how can you remind yourself that God is with you, just like He promised Joshua? What steps can you take today to embrace these changes with courage and trust?

PRAYER

Dear God, thank you for always being with us as we face new changes and challenges. Help us to be strong and brave, just like Joshua, and remind us to trust in Your love and guidance every step of the way.

CHOOSING FAITH OVER FEELINGS

"For we walk by faith, not by sight." 2 Corinthians 5:7

DEVOTIONAL

In life, our feelings can change like the weather. One day, we might feel happy, and the next, sad. But God calls us to trust Him, even when we can't see what's ahead. In 2 Corinthians 5:7, we learn that we walk by faith, not by sight. This means we believe in God's promises, even when we don't feel like it. Today, choose to trust God. Let faith guide your heart, and watch His goodness unfold in your life.

DAILY REFLECTION

Think about a time when your feelings changed quickly, like the weather. How did you respond to those feelings, and how can you choose to trust God in similar situations moving forward?

PRAYER

Dear God, thank you for reminding us that our feelings can change like the weather, but we can always trust in Your loving guidance. Help us to walk by faith, believing in Your promises, even when our hearts feel unsure, and let us find peace in knowing You're with us every step of the way.

THE GOD WHO SEES YOU

"For you created my inmost being; you knit me together in my mother's womb." Psalm 139:13

DEVOTIONAL

God is always with you, watching over you like a loving parent. Psalm 139:13 tells us that God created you just the way you are, knitting you together in your mother's womb. This means He knows you deeply—your feelings, dreams, and even your fears. Whenever you feel alone or unsure, remember that God sees you and loves you. Talk to Him in prayer, and feel His presence as you grow and discover the incredible person He made you to be.

DAILY REFLECTION

Reflect on a time when you felt alone or unsure about yourself. How did it feel to remember that God knows you deeply and is always with you? Take a moment to write down your thoughts and feelings, and consider how you can invite God into that experience through prayer. What does it mean to you to know that you are uniquely made and loved by Him?

PRAYER

Dear God, thank you for always being with me like a loving parent, watching over me and knowing my heart. Help me to remember that I am wonderfully made and that your love surrounds me every day, giving me strength to be myself.

LOVING OTHERS FROM A FULL HEART

"Let all that you do be done in love." 1 Corinthians 16:14

DEVOTIONAL

In everything we do, let's remember to do it with love! Loving others from a full heart means showing kindness and care, even when it's hard. Imagine how you feel when someone is nice to you—now think about how you can make others feel the same way. When we act with love, we brighten the world around us and draw closer to God's heart. Today, ask God to fill your heart with His love, so you can share it freely.

DAILY REFLECTION

Think about a time when someone showed you kindness and love. How did it make you feel? Now, can you think of a way to share that same kindness with someone else today?

PRAYER

Dear God, fill my heart with Your love so I can share kindness with everyone I meet today. Help me remember how wonderful it feels to receive love, and inspire me to brighten someone else's day with a caring word or action.

WAITING WELL WITH GOD

"But those who hope in the Lord will renew their strength. They will soar on wings like eagles; they will run and not grow weary, they will walk and not be faint." Isaiah 40:31

DEVOTIONAL

Waiting can be hard, but it's a special time with God. Isaiah 40:31 reminds us that when we hope in the Lord, He gives us strength to keep going. Think of an eagle soaring high in the sky; we can rise above our worries, too! When we trust God while we wait, He helps us stay strong and joyful. So, let's take a deep breath, pray, and remember that God is always with us, making our hearts lighter.

DAILY REFLECTION

Reflect on a time when you had to wait for something important. How did you feel during that time? In what ways did you see God's presence with you? Take a moment to write down your thoughts and feelings about that experience, and consider how trusting in Him helped you stay strong.

PRAYER

Dear God, thank you for being with us in our waiting times, reminding us that we can find strength and joy when we trust in You. Help us to feel Your presence and lift our hearts high like eagles as we wait for the good things You have planned for us.

LETTING GO OF CONTROL

"Cast all your anxiety on him because he cares for you." 1 Peter 5:7

DEVOTIONAL

Sometimes, we try to hold onto everything—our worries, our plans, and our fears. But 1 Peter 5:7 reminds us to let go of that control and trust God. When we cast our anxiety on Him, we discover His caring presence. Imagine giving a heavy backpack to a friend; it feels lighter, doesn't it? God wants us to share our burdens with Him. Today, take a moment to release your worries to God and feel the freedom that comes from trusting Him.

DAILY REFLECTION

What are some worries or fears you can imagine giving to God today, and how would it feel to let go of those burdens?

PRAYER

Dear God, thank you for being a loving friend who cares for us and helps us carry our worries. Please help us to let go of our fears and trust in Your goodness, knowing that we can find peace in Your loving presence.

GOD'S MERCY IS NEW EACH MORNING

"The steadfast love of the Lord never ceases; his mercies never come to an end; they are new every morning; great is your faithfulness." Lamentations 3:22-23

DEVOTIONAL

Every morning is a special gift from God. Just like the sun rises to start a new day, God's mercy shines on us, fresh and full of love. Lamentations 3:22-23 reminds us that His kindness never runs out; it begins again every day. When we wake up, we can choose to feel thankful for His love. Let's take a moment to remember that God is always faithful, ready to help us in our journey of faith.

DAILY REFLECTION

Reflect on a moment when you felt thankful for something in your life. How can you carry that sense of gratitude with you and recognize God's love and mercy in your daily experiences?

PRAYER

Dear God, thank you for the beautiful gift of each day and for the love and mercy that surrounds us like the warm sunlight. Help us to remember your kindness in every moment, so we can carry gratitude in our hearts and share your love with those we meet.

WALKING IN CONFIDENCE, NOT COMPARISON

"For we are God's masterpiece, created in Christ Jesus to do good works, which God prepared in advance for us to do." Ephesians 2:10

DEVOTIONAL

God made you special, just like a beautiful masterpiece. Ephesians 2:10 tells us that you are created in Christ to do wonderful things! Sometimes, we might look at others and feel like we don't measure up. But remember, God has a unique plan just for you. Instead of comparing ourselves to others, let's focus on the good things God has for us. Trust that you are perfect just the way you are, made to shine in your own way!

DAILY REFLECTION

When you think about being a unique masterpiece that God created, what are some special qualities or talents you see in yourself that help you shine? How can you use those gifts to help others and make a difference?

PRAYER

Dear God, thank You for making me special like a beautiful masterpiece, full of unique talents and qualities. Help me to see the gifts You've given me and to use them to shine brightly and make a difference in the world around me.

WHEN PRAYERS GO UNANSWERED

"Be joyful in hope, patient in affliction, faithful in prayer." Romans 12:12

DEVOTIONAL

Sometimes, it feels like our prayers go unanswered, making us wonder if God is listening. Romans 12:12 reminds us to "be joyful in hope, patient in affliction, and faithful in prayer." This means we should keep trusting God, even when things are tough. Like a seed that takes time to grow, our prayers need patience to bloom. Remember, God loves you and is with you in every moment. Stay hopeful, keep praying, and let His love guide you.

DAILY REFLECTION

Reflect on a time when you felt your prayers were unanswered. How did it affect your hope and patience during that period? What steps can you take to continue trusting God, even when things seem tough?

PRAYER

Dear God, even when it feels like our prayers are quiet, help us remember that You are always listening and loving us. Give us the strength to be joyful, patient, and faithful, trusting that in Your perfect time, our hopes will blossom.

FINDING JOY IN GOD ALONE

"Delight yourself in the Lord, and he will grant you the desires of your heart." Psalm 37:4

DEVOTIONAL

Finding joy in God means trusting Him with our hearts. Psalm 37:4 tells us to delight in the Lord. This means spending time with Him in prayer, reading His Word, and enjoying His creation. When we fill our hearts with His love, our desires change to what truly matters. As we grow closer to God, we discover joy that nothing else can bring. Let's seek Him first, and watch how He fills our hearts with happiness!

DAILY REFLECTION

Reflecting on the message about finding joy in God, how can you spend time with Him this week in ways that make your heart feel happy and full? Consider activities like prayer, reading a Bible passage, or enjoying a moment in nature. What specific actions can you take to draw closer to Him and experience the joy He offers?

PRAYER

Dear God, help us to delight in You and trust You with our hearts, filling us with joy that comes from spending time in Your Word and creation. May we seek You each day, finding happiness in Your love and growing closer to You in everything we do.

YOUR LIFE STILL HAS PURPOSE

"For I know the plans I have for you, declares the Lord, plans to prosper you and not to harm you, plans to give you hope and a future." Jeremiah 29:11

DEVOTIONAL

God loves you and has a special plan for your life! Even when things feel tough or confusing, remember that you have a purpose. Just like a beautiful puzzle, each piece of your life fits together for something wonderful. Jeremiah 29:11 reminds us that God wants to give you hope and a bright future. Talk to Him about your dreams and fears. Trust that He will guide you and help you grow every day!

DAILY REFLECTION

What is one dream or hope you can talk to God about today, knowing that He has a special plan for your life? How can you trust Him to help you with any feelings of confusion or uncertainty you may have?

PRAYER

Dear God, thank you for loving me and reminding me that I have a special purpose in my life. Please help me trust in Your plan, especially when things feel confusing or tough, and guide me as I share my dreams and hopes with You.

SPEAKING LIFE OVER YOURSELF

"Death and life are in the power of the tongue, and those who love it will eat its fruits." Proverbs 18:21

DEVOTIONAL

Every word you speak has power! In Proverbs 18:21, we learn that our tongue can bring life or death. When you say kind, encouraging things about yourself, you fill your heart with joy and hope. Instead of thinking, "I can't do this," say, "I am strong and brave!" Speak words that reflect God's love for you. Remember, you are special and capable. Let your words lift you up and help you shine bright for others to see!

DAILY REFLECTION

Reflect on a time when you spoke something kind or encouraging to yourself. How did it make you feel? Now, think of a situation where you found it hard to be kind to yourself. What positive words could you say instead to support yourself in that moment?

PRAYER

Dear God, thank You for the amazing power of my words; help me always to speak kindly to myself and others, reminding me of the love You have for each of us. When I feel unsure, gently guide my heart to say, "I am strong and brave," so that I may shine Your light and share joy with the world.

WHEN YOU FEEL SPIRITUALLY DRY

"He restores my soul; He leads me in paths of righteousness for His name's sake." Psalm 23:3

DEVOTIONAL

When you feel spiritually dry, remember that God cares for you deeply. Just like a thirsty plant needs water, your soul needs His refreshing love. Psalm 23:3 reminds us that God restores our souls and guides us on the right paths. When you're feeling empty, take a moment to pray or read your Bible. God is always there, ready to fill you with joy and peace. Trust Him to lead you back to a place of hope and strength.

DAILY REFLECTION

When you find yourself feeling spiritually dry, how can you create a space in your day to connect with God and seek His refreshing love?

PRAYER

Dear God, thank You for always caring for me and for the love that fills my heart. Please help me to take a moment to connect with You, so I can feel Your refreshing presence and find hope and strength in my spirit.

HEALED BY HIS WORD

"He sent His word and healed them, and delivered them from their destructions."
Psalm 107:20

DEVOTIONAL

God's Word is powerful! Psalm 107:20 tells us that He sent His Word to heal and save us. When we read the Bible and listen to God, we feel comforted and renewed. If we're sad, worried, or hurt, His words can bring peace and hope. Take a moment each day to read a verse and let it fill your heart with His love. Remember, God's Word is a gift that helps us grow closer to Him.

DAILY REFLECTION

Reflect on a time when you felt comforted or renewed after reading a verse from the Bible. What did that verse mean to you, and how did it help you during a difficult moment? How can you make reading God's Word a part of your daily routine to continue experiencing His peace and hope?

PRAYER

Dear God, thank you for giving us Your Word, which brings healing and comfort to our hearts. Help us to remember to spend time reading it each day, so we can feel Your love and find peace, especially when we are feeling sad or worried.

GOD'S LOVE THAT NEVER FAILS

"For I am convinced that neither death nor life, neither angels nor demons, neither the present nor the future, nor any powers, will be able to separate us from the love of God that is in Christ Jesus our Lord." Romans 8:38-39

DEVOTIONAL

God's love is like a strong, warm hug that never lets go. In Romans 8:38-39, we learn that nothing can separate us from this love—not even the scariest things like death or the unknown future. Imagine a big blanket wrapping around you, keeping you safe and secure. No matter what happens in life, remember that God loves you deeply and completely. Each day, talk to Him, and let that love fill your heart with joy and peace.

DAILY REFLECTION

How does knowing that God's love wraps around you like a warm blanket make you feel safe and secure in your everyday life? Take a moment to think about a time when you felt scared or uncertain. How can remembering God's love help you in those moments?

PRAYER

Dear God, thank you for your love that wraps around me like a warm, cozy blanket, always keeping me safe and secure. Help me remember that no matter what happens, your love is there, giving me joy and peace when I feel scared or uncertain.

OVERFLOWING WITH GRATITUDE

"Give thanks in all circumstances; for this is the will of God in Christ Jesus for you."
1 Thessalonians 5:18

DEVOTIONAL

In all moments, big or small, we have reasons to be thankful. 1 Thessalonians 5:18 reminds us to give thanks in every circumstance. When we recognize the good things God provides—friends, family, nature, or even a warm meal—we start to feel our hearts fill with joy. Gratitude helps us see God's love and care in our lives. Today, take a moment to thank God for the blessings around you. Let your thankfulness overflow!

DAILY REFLECTION

Reflect on your day and consider the moments, both big and small, that brought you joy. What are three things you can be thankful for right now? How do these blessings remind you of God's love and care in your life? Take a moment to express your gratitude to God for these gifts.

PRAYER

Dear God, thank you for the countless blessings you fill our lives with each day, from the laughter of friends to the beauty of nature. Help us to see your love in every moment and to let our hearts overflow with gratitude for all the good things you provide.

FORGIVING YOURSELF AND OTHERS

"Be kind and compassionate to one another, forgiving each other, just as in Christ God forgave you." Ephesians 4:32

DEVOTIONAL

Forgiveness is a beautiful gift. Sometimes, we hurt others or even ourselves, and it's easy to feel sad or angry. But God wants us to be kind and compassionate, just like Him. When we forgive, we let go of those bad feelings and make space for love and joy. Remember, God forgives us, and we can do the same for ourselves and others. Today, try to let go of any hurt and choose to forgive.

DAILY REFLECTION

Think about a time when you felt hurt or sad because of something that happened. How would it feel to let go of that hurt and choose to forgive? What kind or loving action might you take today to show forgiveness to yourself or someone else?

PRAYER

Dear God, thank you for the beautiful gift of forgiveness that helps us release our hurt and embrace love and joy. Please guide us to let go of our sadness and choose kindness, so we can show compassion to ourselves and others today.

GOD'S STRENGTH IN YOUR WEAKNESS

"My grace is sufficient for you, for my power is made perfect in weakness." 2 Corinthians 12:9

DEVOTIONAL

When we feel weak or unsure, it can be hard to remember that God's strength is always with us. In 2 Corinthians 12:9, we learn that God's grace is enough for us. This means that even when we feel small or alone, God's power shines through our struggles. When things are tough, we can ask Him for help. Trust that He will lift you up. Each day, rely on His strength, knowing He is always by your side.

DAILY REFLECTION

Reflect on a time when you felt weak or unsure. What did you do in that situation, and how can you remember to ask for God's strength when challenges arise in the future?

PRAYER

Dear God, when we feel weak and unsure, help us to remember that Your strength is always with us, lifting us up in our times of need. Teach us to trust in Your grace and ask for Your help, knowing that Your power shines through our struggles, guiding us each step of the way.

ANXIOUS FOR NOTHING

"Do not be anxious about anything, but in every situation, by prayer and petition, with thanksgiving, present your requests to God." Philippians 4:6

DEVOTIONAL

When you feel worried or scared, remember what God says in Philippians 4:6: "Do not be anxious about anything." Instead of letting worries take over, talk to God in prayer. Share what's on your mind, and thank Him for what you have. God loves to hear from you! Each time you pray, you'll find comfort and peace. Trust that God is in control, and know that He will help you through anything that makes you anxious.

DAILY REFLECTION

When you feel worried or scared, how can you remind yourself to turn your thoughts to prayer and gratitude instead of letting anxiety take over? What are some specific things you can talk to God about when you're feeling this way?

PRAYER

Dear God, when I feel worried or scared, help me remember to talk to You and share what's on my heart. Thank You for listening and for all the good things in my life; I trust that You are always with me, bringing me peace.

LIVING A LEGACY OF FAITH

"Let your light shine before others, that they may see your good deeds and glorify your Father in heaven." Matthew 5:16

DEVOTIONAL

Every day, you have a chance to share your light with others! Remember Matthew 5:16, where Jesus encourages us to let our light shine. This means showing kindness, helping those in need, and being a friend. When you do good things, others notice and may even want to know about God's love. Your actions can inspire them! As you live with love and compassion, you are creating a beautiful legacy of faith. Let your light shine bright!

DAILY REFLECTION

How can you share your light with someone today by being kind or helpful? Think of one simple action you can take to show love and compassion to others.

PRAYER

Dear God, help me to shine my light brightly by being kind and helpful to those around me. May my small acts of love bring joy to others and show them your wonderful love.

PEACE IN THE MIDST OF CHANGE

"Be still, and know that I am God." Psalm 46:10

DEVOTIONAL

Change can feel overwhelming, but in those moments, God invites us to find peace. Psalm 46:10 reminds us to "Be still, and know that I am God." When life gets busy or confusing, take a deep breath. Close your eyes and remember that God is in control. Trust Him to guide you through every change. In the stillness, you'll discover His love and strength, helping you grow closer to Him each day. Find peace in His presence.

DAILY REFLECTION

When you feel overwhelmed by change, what are some specific ways you can pause, be still, and remind yourself that God is in control?

PRAYER

Dear God, when the changes around me feel too big and overwhelming, help me to pause, take a deep breath, and remember that You are always in control. In those quiet moments, fill my heart with Your peace, reminding me of Your love and strength as I trust You to guide me through each new day.

WHEN YOU FEEL INADEQUATE

"But he said to me, 'My grace is sufficient for you, for my power is made perfect in weakness.'" 2 Corinthians 12:9

DEVOTIONAL

When you feel inadequate, remember that it's okay to be weak sometimes. The Bible tells us that God's grace is enough for us. This means that when we feel like we can't do something, God's strength helps us. Instead of focusing on what we lack, we can trust that God will support us through tough times. Let His love fill you up, and know that it's in our weaknesses that His power shines brightest. Keep trusting Him!

DAILY REFLECTION

When you feel weak or unsure of yourself, how can you remind yourself of God's grace and strength in your life? Think of a moment when you relied on Him, and how that made you feel supported.

PRAYER

Dear God, thank You for Your unwavering love that reminds us it's okay to feel weak sometimes, for in our struggles, we find Your strength. Help us to trust in Your grace, remembering the times You have supported us, so we can shine bright even when we feel unsure.

GOD IS YOUR REFUGE

"God is our refuge and strength, a very present help in trouble." Psalm 46:1

DEVOTIONAL

When we face hard times, it's easy to feel scared or alone. But Psalm 46:1 reminds us that God is like a warm, strong shelter we can run to. When life gets tough, we can talk to God and ask for help. He listens and cares for us. Remember, no matter what troubles come your way, God is always there to support and protect you. Trust Him, and let Him be your safe place.

DAILY REFLECTION

How can you remind yourself to turn to God as your safe place when you're feeling scared or alone? What are some ways you can talk to Him about your worries?

PRAYER

Dear God, thank you for being our safe place when we feel scared or alone. Help us to remember to talk to you about our worries, knowing that you always listen and care for us.

CHOOSING OBEDIENCE OVER COMFORT

"For we walk by faith, not by sight." 2 Corinthians 5:7

DEVOTIONAL

Choosing obedience over comfort can be tough, but it's the path that leads us closer to God. In 2 Corinthians 5:7, we learn that we walk by faith, not by sight. This means we trust God even when we can't see His plan. Imagine being asked to take a step forward in the dark. It's scary, but if we obey, we find God waiting to guide us. Let's choose to follow Him today and see how He lights our way!

DAILY REFLECTION

Think about a time when you faced a choice between doing what felt comfortable and being obedient to what you felt was right. How did you feel in that moment, and what decision did you make? How can you take a step of faith today by choosing obedience, even if it feels a little scary?

PRAYER

Dear God, help us to choose obedience over comfort, trusting that you have a wonderful plan for us, even when the path seems unclear. Give us the courage to take steps of faith today, knowing that you are always there to guide us with your loving light.

BE STILL AND KNOW

"Be still, and know that I am God." Psalm 46:10

DEVOTIONAL

In the busy moments of life, it's easy to forget that God is always with us. Psalm 46:10 reminds us to "Be still, and know that I am God." This means taking time to pause, breathe, and listen. When we quiet our hearts, we can feel God's love and hear His voice guiding us. Remember, it's in the silence that we grow closer to Him. Take a moment today to be still and trust in His presence.

DAILY REFLECTION

Take a moment to think about a time in your life when you felt overwhelmed or busy. How can you create space in your day to pause, be still, and connect with God? What does being still mean to you in those hectic moments?

PRAYER

Dear God, in the rush of our busy days, help us to remember to pause and feel Your presence around us. Teach us to be still, so we can hear Your gentle voice guiding us with love and peace.

PRESSING ON WHEN YOU'RE WEARY

"But those who hope in the Lord will renew their strength. They will soar on wings like eagles; they will run and not grow weary, they will walk and not be faint." Isaiah 40:31

DEVOTIONAL

When you feel tired and worn out, remember God's promise in Isaiah 40:31. He invites us to hope in Him, and He will give us strength. Imagine soaring like an eagle, free and strong, or running a race without getting tired. God helps us move forward, even when we're weary. Whenever you feel overwhelmed, take a moment to pray. Lean on Him, and watch how He fills you with joy and energy to keep going!

DAILY REFLECTION

When you feel tired or overwhelmed, how can you remember to take a moment to pray and ask God for strength? What might that prayer look like, and how do you think it could help you feel better?

PRAYER

Dear God, when I feel tired and heavy, help me to remember to pause and reach out to You, trusting in Your promise to give me strength. Please fill my heart with Your joy and energy, so I can keep moving forward with a light spirit and renewed hope.

GOD'S GENTLE CORRECTION

"For the Lord disciplines those he loves, and he chastises everyone he accepts as his son." Hebrews 12:6

DEVOTIONAL

God loves us so much that He wants us to grow and be our best. Sometimes, this means He helps us learn through gentle correction, just like a loving parent guides a child. Hebrews 12:6 reminds us that God's discipline shows us His love and helps us become stronger. When we make mistakes, instead of feeling sad, we can remember that God is helping us learn and grow closer to Him. Trust in His loving guidance each day.

DAILY REFLECTION

Think about a time when you made a mistake or faced a challenge. How did that experience help you grow or learn something new? In what ways can you see God's loving guidance in those moments?

PRAYER

Dear God, thank You for loving us so completely and helping us grow into the best versions of ourselves. When we make mistakes or face challenges, please remind us that Your gentle guidance helps us learn and strengthens our hearts.

HOPE THAT WILL NOT DISAPPOINT

"For I know the plans I have for you, declares the Lord, plans to prosper you and not to harm you, plans to give you hope and a future." Jeremiah 29:11

DEVOTIONAL

God has wonderful plans for you, full of hope and love. Sometimes, life can be hard, and we might feel lost or worried. But remember, God is always with you! He knows your future and wants to guide you to good things. Trust in Him, and believe that every day is part of His special plan for you. Keep praying and reading the Bible, and you will feel His love and hope shining in your life.

DAILY REFLECTION

How does knowing that God has a special plan for you make you feel, especially on days when you feel lost or worried?

PRAYER

Dear God, thank you for having wonderful plans for me, filled with hope and love. When I feel lost or worried, help me remember that you are always with me, guiding my path and filling my heart with your peace.

BECOMING MORE LIKE CHRIST

"And we all, who with unveiled faces contemplate the Lord's glory, are being transformed into his image with ever-increasing glory, which comes from the Lord, who is the Spirit." - 2 Corinthians 3:18

DEVOTIONAL

As we look at Jesus and learn about His love, kindness, and patience, we start to change. Just like a butterfly transforms from a caterpillar, we are made more like Christ every day. When we spend time with God through prayer and reading the Bible, His Spirit helps us grow. Remember, each small step you take brings you closer to His light. Let's choose to reflect His love and grace in everything we do!

DAILY REFLECTION

How can you show kindness and love to someone this week, reflecting the way Jesus cares for us?

PRAYER

Dear God, thank you for showing us Your love and kindness through Jesus. Help us to remember that as we grow closer to You, we can share that same love and kindness with others, just like a beautiful butterfly spreading its wings.

FAITH OVER FEAR

"For God has not given us a spirit of fear, but of power and of love and of a sound mind." 2 Timothy 1:7

DEVOTIONAL

When we feel scared, it's easy to let those feelings take over. But remember, God gives us strength and love instead of fear. 2 Timothy 1:7 reminds us that we have a powerful spirit within us. When worry creeps in, pray and ask God for courage. He helps us think clearly and makes our hearts brave. Trust in His love, and let faith shine brighter than your fears. You can always find strength in God!

DAILY REFLECTION

How do you feel when you experience fear or worry, and in what ways can you remind yourself to trust in God's love and strength during those moments?

PRAYER

Dear God, when I feel scared or worried, help me remember that Your love gives me strength and courage. Please fill my heart with Your peace, so I can trust in You and let my faith shine bright, even when fear tries to sneak in.

WHEN GOD FEELS SILENT

"I will never leave you nor forsake you." Hebrews 13:5

DEVOTIONAL

Sometimes, it feels like God is quiet, and we wonder if He is really with us. But Hebrews 13:5 reminds us that God promises, "I will never leave you nor forsake you." Even when we can't hear Him, He is still by our side, caring for us. In these moments, we can pray, read the Bible, or spend time in nature to connect with Him. Remember, His love is always there, even when it's hard to feel.

DAILY REFLECTION

When you feel like God is quiet and it seems hard to connect with Him, what are some things you can do to remind yourself of His presence and love?

PRAYER

Dear God, even when it feels like You are quiet and we're not sure if You are near, help us to remember Your promise to always be with us. May we find comfort in Your love, seek You through prayer, and feel Your presence in the beauty of nature around us.

BECOMING A VESSEL OF GRACE

"But we have this treasure in jars of clay, to show that the surpassing power belongs to God and not to us." 2 Corinthians 4:7

DEVOTIONAL

In 2 Corinthians 4:7, Paul tells us that we are like jars of clay, holding God's amazing treasures. These treasures are His love, kindness, and grace. While we may feel weak or flawed, God uses us to show His great power. Think of how a simple jar can hold something beautiful! Today, ask God to fill you with His grace so you can share it with others. Remember, your heart can shine brightly with His love, no matter your imperfections.

DAILY REFLECTION

As you think about being a jar of clay filled with God's treasures, what is one way you can share His love or grace with someone today, even if you feel imperfect or weak?

PRAYER

Dear God, thank You for creating us as beautiful jars of clay filled with Your love and grace. Help us to share Your treasures with others today, reminding us that even when we feel imperfect, our hearts can shine with Your light.

LEARNING TO DEPEND ON HIM

"Trust in the Lord with all your heart and lean not on your own understanding." Proverbs 3:5

DEVOTIONAL

Trusting God means believing He knows what's best for us, even when we don't understand. Proverbs 3:5 reminds us to rely on Him completely. Think of a time when you were unsure or worried—maybe about school or friends. Instead of leaning on your own thoughts, try praying and asking God for help. He loves you and wants to guide you. Each day, practice trusting Him more, knowing He is always there to support you on your journey.

DAILY REFLECTION

Reflect on a time when you felt uncertain or worried about something in your life. How did you handle those feelings? Take a moment to think about how you can trust God more in similar situations moving forward. What specific steps can you take to lean on Him and seek His guidance when you're feeling uncertain?

PRAYER

Dear God, thank You for loving me and guiding me even when I feel unsure or worried. Help me to trust in Your wisdom and lean on You for support, knowing that You always have my best interests at heart.

GOD'S TIMING IS PERFECT

"To everything there is a season, a time for every purpose under heaven."
Ecclesiastes 3:1

DEVOTIONAL

God's timing is always perfect! The Bible tells us in Ecclesiastes 3:1 that "To everything there is a season, a time for every purpose under heaven." Sometimes we feel like things should happen right away, but God knows the best time for everything in our lives. Just like a beautiful flower blooms at the right moment, so will our dreams and prayers. Trust Him! Remember, waiting can be a special time to grow closer to God.

DAILY REFLECTION

Think about a time when you had to wait for something you really wanted. How did you feel during that waiting period, and what did you learn about trusting God's timing?

PRAYER

Dear God, thank you for reminding us that you have a perfect plan and timing for everything in our lives. Help us to trust you while we wait, knowing that, just like a flower blooms in your time, our dreams will also unfold beautifully when the moment is right.

YOU ARE NOT ALONE

"For I am convinced that neither death nor life, neither angels nor demons, neither the present nor the future, nor any powers, will be able to separate us from the love of God." Romans 8:38-39

DEVOTIONAL

You are never alone. No matter what happens in your life—good or bad—God's love is always with you. Romans 8:38-39 reminds us that nothing can separate us from His love. When you feel scared or lonely, remember that God is right beside you, caring for you. Talk to Him through prayer; share your fears and joys. As you grow in faith, know that His love surrounds you, giving you strength and comfort every day.

DAILY REFLECTION

Think about a time when you felt scared or lonely. How did remembering that God is always with you change how you felt in that moment? What are some ways you can talk to God about your fears and joys today?

PRAYER

Dear God, thank you for being with me always, even when I feel scared or lonely. Help me to remember that your love surrounds me and to share my fears and joys with you in prayer.

ABIDING IN THE VINE

"I am the vine; you are the branches. Whoever abides in me and I in him, he it is that bears much fruit, for apart from me you can do nothing." John 15:5

DEVOTIONAL

Jesus tells us He is the vine, and we are the branches. When we stay close to Him, we can grow and be strong, just like a tree in a garden. If we stay connected by praying, reading the Bible, and loving others, we will bear good fruit, like kindness and joy. Remember, without Him, we can't do much at all. Let's choose to abide in Jesus every day, growing in faith and sharing His love with the world!

DAILY REFLECTION

How can you practice staying connected to Jesus today, so you can show love and kindness to others, just like a branch connected to a strong vine?

PRAYER

Dear Jesus, thank you for being our strong vine, helping us grow and bear good fruit in our hearts. Please guide us to stay close to you each day, so we can share love and kindness with everyone around us.

TRUSTING THROUGH TRANSITIONS

"Trust in the Lord with all your heart and lean not on your own understanding." Proverbs 3:5

DEVOTIONAL

As we go through different changes in life, it can feel scary. But God wants us to trust Him, even when we don't understand everything. Proverbs 3:5 reminds us to believe in the Lord with all our heart. This means looking to Him for help instead of relying on our own thoughts. When things feel uncertain, take a moment to pray and ask God for guidance. Remember, He is always with you, leading you toward good things.

DAILY REFLECTION

When you feel unsure or scared about changes in your life, how can you remind yourself to trust God and ask for His guidance?

PRAYER

Dear God, thank You for always being with us, even when life feels uncertain and scary. Help us to trust You fully and remember to look to You for guidance as we navigate the changes that come our way.

CHOOSING PEACE IN UNCERTAINTY

"Peace I leave with you; my peace I give you." John 14:27

DEVOTIONAL

In John 14:27, Jesus offers us a special gift—His peace. When life feels uncertain or confusing, we can remember that Jesus is always with us. Choosing to trust Him means we can find calm even in the storm. Take a deep breath and say a quiet prayer, asking for His peace to fill your heart. Remember, you are not alone; God is always by your side, guiding you through every worry. Embrace His peace today!

DAILY REFLECTION

How can you invite Jesus' peace into your life during times when you feel worried or unsure? Take a moment to think about a specific situation and what it would look like to trust Him in that moment.

PRAYER

Dear Jesus, thank you for your loving promise of peace in our hearts, especially when life feels confusing or uncertain. Help me to trust in you more deeply, so that I can feel your calm presence guiding me through every worry and doubt.

HOLDING ON TO GOD'S PROMISES

"For all the promises of God in Him are Yes, and in Him Amen, to the glory of God through us." 2 Corinthians 1:20

DEVOTIONAL

God makes lots of promises to us, and He always keeps them! In 2 Corinthians 1:20, we learn that everything God says is true. When we feel scared or worried, we can remember that God is always with us and will help us. Holding on to His promises means trusting that He has good plans for us. When we believe in His words and look for His goodness, we grow closer to Him and feel His love every day.

DAILY REFLECTION

Think about a time when you felt scared or worried. How can remembering God's promises help you feel better and trust that He is with you?

PRAYER

Dear God, thank You for always keeping Your promises and for being with us when we feel scared or worried. Help us to trust in Your goodness and remember that Your words are true, so we can feel Your love guiding us every day.

LETTING GOD DEFINE YOUR WORTH

"You are precious and honored in my sight, and I love you."
Isaiah 43:4

DEVOTIONAL

You are so special to God! Isaiah 43:4 reminds us, "You are precious and honored in my sight, and I love you." When we feel unsure about our worth, we can remember that God's love makes us valuable. Your worth isn't based on how well you do at school or what others think of you; it's defined by God's love for you. Today, take a moment to thank God for loving you just as you are. You are His treasure!

DAILY REFLECTION

Reflect for a moment: How does knowing that you are precious and loved by God change the way you see yourself and your worth? Take some time to write down or share with someone what makes you feel valued and loved, just as you are.

PRAYER

Dear God, thank You for loving me exactly as I am and for reminding me that I am precious to You. Help me to see my true worth through Your eyes, so that I can feel valued and cherished every day.

ENCOURAGEMENT FOR THE WEARY SOUL

"Come to me, all you who are weary and burdened, and I will give you rest."
Matthew 11:28

DEVOTIONAL

When you feel tired or overwhelmed, remember Jesus' words in Matthew 11:28: "Come to me, all you who are weary and burdened, and I will give you rest." This promise is a gentle reminder that you don't have to carry your struggles alone. Jesus invites you to share your worries with Him. Take a moment to stop, pray, and rest in His love. Trust that He will refresh your spirit and give you the strength you need.

DAILY REFLECTION

Reflect on a time when you felt tired or overwhelmed. How did you handle those feelings? Take a moment to think about how inviting Jesus into your struggles could change your perspective. What worries or burdens would you like to share with Him today? Remember His promise of rest and strength, and spend some time in prayer, asking for His support. How can you actively seek His presence in your daily life?

PRAYER

Dear Jesus, when I feel tired or overwhelmed, help me remember that I can come to You with my worries and burdens, trusting in Your promise to give me rest. Please refresh my spirit and fill me with Your love and strength, guiding me through the struggles I face today.

WHEN YOU FEEL SPIRITUALLY STUCK

"Cast all your anxiety on him because he cares for you." 1 Peter 5:7

DEVOTIONAL

When you feel spiritually stuck, remember that God is always there for you. In 1 Peter 5:7, we learn to cast our worries on Him because He truly cares. Imagine giving your anxieties to God like handing Him a heavy backpack. He wants to help lighten your load! Take a moment to pray, share your feelings, and listen for His comfort. Trust that He is guiding you, and in that trust, you will find renewed strength and purpose.

DAILY REFLECTION

When you think about the heavy things you carry, what worries or feelings would you like to hand over to God right now? Consider how it would feel to let go of that weight and trust that He is taking care of you.

PRAYER

Dear God, I come to you with my worries and feelings that sometimes feel too heavy to carry. Please help me to trust in Your love and let go of these burdens, knowing You are always here to lighten my load and guide me.

FAITH THAT MOVES MOUNTAINS

"If you have faith as small as a mustard seed, you can say to this mountain, 'Move from here to there,' and it will move." Matthew 17:20

DEVOTIONAL

Faith can be as tiny as a mustard seed, but even that small faith is powerful. Think about a mountain—big and strong. Jesus tells us that with just a little faith, we can ask God to move mountains in our lives. This means trusting God to help us with our problems, big or small. When we believe in Him, He can do amazing things! Start today by trusting God with your worries and watch how He works wonders.

DAILY REFLECTION

When you think about something in your life that feels as big as a mountain, what is one small way you can trust God with that worry today?

PRAYER

Dear God, thank you for reminding me that even a tiny bit of faith can make a big difference. Help me to trust You with my worries, knowing You can do amazing things in my life, just like moving mountains.

THE GENTLE VOICE OF GOD

"And after the fire came a gentle whisper." 1 Kings 19:12

DEVOTIONAL

In 1 Kings 19:12, we learn about God's gentle whisper that follows a powerful storm. Sometimes, we think God speaks in loud, exciting ways. But often, He quietly reaches our hearts. Take a moment to sit in silence and listen. In those still times, God can share His love and guidance with you. Remember, His gentle voice reminds us that He is always near, wanting to comfort and guide us through our day. Embrace those quiet moments!

DAILY REFLECTION

In the busyness of your day, how can you create a few quiet moments to listen for God's gentle whisper and reflect on His love and guidance in your life?

PRAYER

Dear God, thank you for the gentle whispers of your love that comfort us in quiet moments. Help us find a little time each day to listen for your voice and feel your guidance in our hearts.

LIVING WITH KINGDOM VISION

"Seek first the kingdom of God and His righteousness, and all these things shall be added to you." Matthew 6:33

DEVOTIONAL

God wants us to focus on Him above all else. When we seek His kingdom and do what is right, He promises to take care of our needs. Imagine planting seeds in a garden: if we water the seeds, they grow strong and beautiful. In the same way, when we spend time with God through prayer and reading the Bible, our relationship with Him flourishes. Let's remember to put God first every day, and trust Him to provide for us!

DAILY REFLECTION

How can you make time each day to focus on God and nurture your relationship with Him, just like you would care for a garden?

PRAYER

Dear God, help us to always put You first in our hearts, trusting that when we seek Your kingdom, You will take care of all our needs. Just like we water our garden to help it grow, remind us to spend time with You through prayer and reading, so our love for You blossoms every day.

STANDING FIRM IN FAITH

"Stand firm in the faith; be courageous; be strong."
1 Corinthians 16:13

DEVOTIONAL

When we stand firm in our faith, we show that we trust God, even when things are tough. The Bible tells us to be courageous and strong. This means believing in God and doing the right thing, even when it's hard. Think of a tree that bends but doesn't break in the wind. When we trust God, we can stand tall like that tree. Pray for strength each day, and remember, God is always with you!

DAILY REFLECTION

Reflect on a time when you faced a difficult situation. How did you show courage and trust in God? What helped you to stand firm in your faith, and what can you do in the future to be like the tree that bends but doesn't break?

PRAYER

Dear God, help us to be strong like the tree that bends but doesn't break; give us courage to trust in You when life gets tough. Remind us each day that You are always by our side, ready to help us stand firm in our faith.

LETTING GO OF SHAME

"Therefore, there is now no condemnation for those who are in Christ Jesus." Romans 8:1

DEVOTIONAL

Sometimes we feel burdened by our mistakes, and shame can weigh us down. But Romans 8:1 reminds us that in Jesus, there is no condemnation. This means we are forgiven and loved, no matter what we've done. Imagine letting go of that heavy backpack filled with shame. With each step, we can feel lighter and freer. Trust that God sees you through Jesus and wants you to grow in His love. Embrace His forgiveness and walk in joy!

DAILY REFLECTION

What are some mistakes or burdens you can imagine letting go of today, and how would it feel to walk in the light of forgiveness and love?

PRAYER

Dear God, thank you for your endless love and forgiveness, reminding us that we can let go of our mistakes and burdens just like a heavy backpack we've been carrying. Help us to feel your light and joy in our hearts as we walk freely in your grace, knowing we are cherished just as we are.

March 19

ANCHORED IN HIS WORD

"Your word is a lamp to my feet and a light to my path." Psalm 119:105

DEVOTIONAL

God's Word is like a bright flashlight that guides us through dark places. Just as we need light to see where we're going, we need the Bible to show us the right way to live. When we read the stories and promises in His Word, we learn how to love, forgive, and be kind. Today, let's take a moment to open our Bibles and let God's light shine on our path, helping us grow closer to Him.

DAILY REFLECTION

As you think about how God's Word acts like a flashlight illuminating your path, can you remember a time when a Bible story helped you make a choice or guided you in a difficult situation? How did that make you feel, and what did you learn from it?

PRAYER

Dear God, thank You for Your Word, which lights our way like a bright flashlight in dark places. Help us to open our Bibles and let Your stories and promises guide us, so we can learn to love, forgive, and be kind, growing closer to You each day.

March 20

BRAVE IN THE SMALL THINGS

"Whoever can be trusted with very little can also be trusted with much." Luke 16:10

DEVOTIONAL

Being brave in the small things matters to God! Every day, we have little choices to make. Whether it's being kind to a friend, helping someone in need, or telling the truth, these small acts show our hearts. Jesus teaches us that when we are faithful with little things, He can trust us with bigger ones. Let's pray for courage to do even the tiniest tasks with love, knowing they matter in God's eyes and help us grow closer to Him.

DAILY REFLECTION

Think about a small choice you faced today—maybe it was helping a friend or being honest about something. How did you show bravery in that moment, and how did it make you feel? Take a moment to write down how this act mattered to you and to God.

PRAYER

Dear God, help us to be brave in the small choices we face each day, knowing that even the tiniest acts of kindness and truthfulness matter to You. As we show love in our little actions, may we grow closer to You and learn to trust in the big plans You have for us.

YOUR PAIN HAS A PURPOSE

"And we know that in all things God works for the good of those who love him, who have been called according to his purpose." Romans 8:28

DEVOTIONAL

Sometimes, we face tough times, and it can hurt. But the Bible tells us that God is always with us, working everything for our good (Romans 8:28). When we feel pain, we can remember that God is shaping us, helping us grow stronger in faith. Our struggles can teach us patience, kindness, and trust in Him. So when you're sad or hurt, pray and ask God to show you the purpose in your pain. He cares for you!

DAILY REFLECTION

Reflect on a time when you experienced a tough situation that brought you pain. How did you see God working in that moment, and what did you learn about yourself and your faith through that experience? Write down your thoughts and feelings.

PRAYER

Dear God, thank you for always being with us, even in the tough times that make us feel sad or hurt. Please help us to trust in Your plan and to see the good that comes from our struggles, knowing You are shaping us to be stronger and kinder.

A GOD WHO REDEEMS

"For I know that my Redeemer lives, and that in the end he will stand on the earth." Job 19:25

DEVOTIONAL

In Job 19:25, we find hope in the words "My Redeemer lives." This reminds us that God is always with us, even in tough times. Just as a redeemer helps someone in need, God rescues us from our worries and fears. When we feel sad or alone, we can remember that God is alive and cares deeply for us. Trust that He will stand with us through every challenge we face, guiding and loving us each day.

DAILY REFLECTION

Reflect on a time when you felt worried or alone. How did you sense God's presence during that difficult moment, and how can remembering that "My Redeemer lives" help you face challenges in the future?

PRAYER

Dear God, thank you for being our Redeemer who lives and cares for us, especially when we feel worried or alone. Help us to always remember that you are with us, guiding us through tough times with your love and support.

BECOMING SPIRITUALLY RESILIENT

"I can do all things through Christ who strengthens me." Philippians 4:13

DEVOTIONAL

Life can be tough, and sometimes we feel weak or scared. But remember Philippians 4:13: "I can do all things through Christ who strengthens me." This means that with Jesus by our side, we have the strength to face any challenge! When things get hard, pray and ask Him for help. Trust that He will give you the courage and support you need. Every day, seek to grow closer to Him, and watch how strong you can become!

DAILY REFLECTION

How can you remember to ask Jesus for strength when you're facing something tough, and what steps can you take to grow closer to Him each day?

PRAYER

Dear Jesus, thank you for being our strength when we feel weak or scared; help us to remember that with you by our side, we can face any challenge. Teach us to seek you in our hearts each day, so we can grow closer to you and find the courage we need to overcome life's tough moments.

OVERFLOWING WITH LIVING WATER

"Whoever drinks the water I give them will never thirst; indeed, the water I give them will become in them a spring of water welling up to eternal life." John 4:14

DEVOTIONAL

Imagine drinking water that never runs out! Jesus offers us this special water that fills our hearts and gives us joy forever. When we trust Him, His love flows through us like a spring, helping us share kindness and love with others. Each time we pray or read the Bible, we sip from this endless source. Let's remember to seek Him daily, and let His living water fill us up to overflowing, guiding us on our journey of faith.

DAILY REFLECTION

How does knowing that Jesus offers you a never-ending source of joy and love change the way you think about sharing kindness with others?

PRAYER

Dear Jesus, thank You for the amazing gift of Your never-ending love and joy that fills our hearts like a spring. Help us to trust in You every day so that we can share kindness and love with everyone around us, just like You do.

CHOOSING REST OVER RUSH

"Six days you shall labor, and do all your work, but the seventh day is a Sabbath to the Lord your God." Exodus 20:9-10

DEVOTIONAL

In our busy lives, it's easy to rush through each day, trying to finish everything on our list. But God knows we need rest! He created a special day, a Sabbath, just for us to pause and connect with Him. When we choose to rest and spend time with God, we recharge our hearts and minds. Remember, it's okay to slow down. Let's trust that God will help us with our work when we take time to rest in Him.

DAILY REFLECTION

Reflect on a moment this week when you felt rushed or overwhelmed. How can taking a break or spending time with God this week help you feel more refreshed and connected? What might you do to create a special time of rest in your daily routine?

PRAYER

Dear God, thank you for the special Sabbath you created for us to rest and be with you. Help us to find moments in our busy days to slow down, feel your presence, and recharge our hearts so we can serve others with joy.

A HEART THAT SEEKS GOD

"Blessed are those who hunger and thirst for righteousness, for they shall be satisfied." Matthew 5:6

DEVOTIONAL

In Matthew 5:6, we learn that those who hunger and thirst for what is right will be filled. Just like our bodies need food and water, our hearts need God's love and guidance. When we seek Him through prayer, reading the Bible, or helping others, we grow closer to Him. Let's ask God to fill our hearts with a desire for His goodness each day. As we do, we find true satisfaction in His presence.

DAILY REFLECTION

How can you make time today to seek God's love and goodness, whether through prayer, reading the Bible, or helping someone else? Think about one specific way you can nourish your heart with His presence.

PRAYER

Dear God, help us to feel a deep thirst for Your love and goodness in our hearts every day. As we seek You through prayer, reading Your Word, or helping others, may we be filled with Your peace and joy.

OBEDIENCE IN THE LITTLE THINGS

"And whoever can be trusted with very little can also be trusted with much." Luke 16:10

DEVOTIONAL

In our daily lives, big things often get our attention, but God cares about the small acts of obedience too. When we listen to our parents, help a friend, or follow rules at school, we show our trust in God. Luke 16:10 reminds us that being faithful in little things prepares us for bigger responsibilities. Each small choice matters! Let's make it a habit to do our best in little things, knowing they bring us closer to God and His plans for us.

DAILY REFLECTION

Think of a small act of kindness or obedience you can do today, whether it's helping someone at home or being respectful at school. How do you think this choice reflects your trust in God and prepares you for bigger responsibilities in the future?

PRAYER

Dear God, thank you for reminding us that even the small things we do, like listening to our parents and helping our friends, are important to you. Help us to be faithful in our little choices today, so we can grow closer to you and be ready for the bigger things you have in store for us.

THE GIFT OF QUIET MOMENTS

"Be still, and know that I am God." Psalm 46:10

DEVOTIONAL

In our busy lives, it's easy to forget to pause and listen for God. Psalm 46:10 reminds us, "Be still, and know that I am God." Quiet moments are gifts from God, where we can reflect and feel His presence. When you find a little time to be still—like during a peaceful morning or while watching the clouds—close your eyes and invite God in. These moments help us grow closer to Him and understand His love.

DAILY REFLECTION

When you take a moment to be still and quiet, how does it feel to invite God into that space with you? What thoughts or feelings come to mind when you think about His presence?

PRAYER

Dear God, thank you for the quiet moments in my day, where I can pause and feel your loving presence around me. Help me to remember that when I invite you in, my heart feels calm and my spirit grows closer to you.

HE CARRIES YOUR BURDENS

"Cast your burdens on the LORD, and he will sustain you;"
Psalm 55:22

DEVOTIONAL

Life can feel heavy sometimes, like we're carrying a big backpack filled with worries. But God tells us in Psalm 55:22 to cast our burdens on Him. This means we can share our troubles with God, like telling a friend. When we give Him our worries, He helps lighten our load and gives us strength to keep going. Remember, you're never alone. Trust God to carry your burdens and find comfort in His love every day.

DAILY REFLECTION

What are some worries or burdens you are carrying right now that you can share with God, and how do you think trusting Him with those worries can help you feel lighter and stronger?

PRAYER

Dear God, thank you for letting us share our worries with you, just like we would with a caring friend. Please help me to trust you with my burdens so that I can feel lighter and stronger, knowing you are always there to support me.

YOUR JOURNEY IS SACRED

"For I know the plans I have for you," declares the Lord, "plans to prosper you and not to harm you, plans to give you hope and a future." Jeremiah 29:11

DEVOTIONAL

Your journey is sacred because God has a special plan just for you! Remember, in Jeremiah 29:11, God tells us He has plans for our good, to give us hope and a bright future. Each day is like a new adventure where God walks beside you. Even when things feel tough, trust that He is guiding you. Take a moment to pray and ask God to show you the way. Your faith will grow as you follow Him!

DAILY REFLECTION

Reflect on a time when you felt uncertain or worried about your path. How did you see God guiding you through that experience? What did you learn about His plan for you, and how can you trust Him more in your journey ahead? Take a moment to write or share your thoughts with someone.

PRAYER

Dear God, thank you for being with me on my journey and for having a special plan just for me. Help me trust in You, even when things feel uncertain, and guide me to follow the bright path you have created for my life.

VICTORY IN CHRIST

"But thanks be to God, who gives us the victory through our Lord Jesus Christ." 1 Corinthians 15:57

DEVOTIONAL

Victory in Christ means that no matter what struggles we face, we can find strength and hope in Him. The Bible tells us in 1 Corinthians 15:57 that God gives us victory through Jesus. This means that when we feel weak or afraid, we can remember that Jesus is with us, helping us overcome challenges. Let's thank God for the victory He has given us and trust Him to guide us each day, bringing peace and joy to our hearts.

DAILY REFLECTION

Think about a time when you felt weak or afraid. How can remembering that Jesus is with you give you strength and hope in your current challenges? Take a moment to write or share your thoughts on how you can trust Him to guide you each day.

PRAYER

Dear God, thank You for the victory we have in Jesus, reminding us that even when we feel weak or afraid, You are always with us, providing strength and hope. Help us to trust in Your guidance each day and to find peace and joy in Your loving presence.

RENEWAL IN CHRIST

"Therefore, if anyone is in Christ, the new creation has come: The old has gone, the new is here!" 2 Corinthians 5:17

DEVOTIONAL

Every day is a chance for a fresh start in Christ. When we believe in Him, we become new creations! This means our past mistakes and worries can be left behind, and we can embrace hope and joy. Picture a caterpillar transforming into a beautiful butterfly. Just like that, God changes us from the inside out. Let's thank Him for the new life we have and ask Him to help us grow more like Him each day.

DAILY REFLECTION

As you think about the idea of being a new creation in Christ, what is one thing from your past that you can choose to let go of today to embrace the fresh start God offers you? How can you open your heart to grow more like Him in this new season?

PRAYER

Dear God, thank you for the fresh start you give us each day as we become new creations in Christ. Help us to let go of our past mistakes and worries, and guide us to grow more like You, embracing the hope and joy that comes with knowing You.

WHEN YOU NEED REASSURANCE

"Fear not, for I am with you; be not dismayed, for I am your God; I will strengthen you, I will help you, I will uphold you with my righteous right hand." Isaiah 41:10

DEVOTIONAL

Sometimes, we all feel scared or unsure. But remember Isaiah 41:10—it reminds us that God is always with us. When you feel afraid, take a moment to pray and ask God for strength. He promises to help and support you, just like a loving parent. Trust that you are never alone; God lifts you up with His strong hand. Every day can be filled with courage and joy if you remember that God is by your side.

DAILY REFLECTION

Think about a time when you felt scared or unsure. How did you feel in that moment, and what helped you feel better? Take a moment to pray and ask God for strength, remembering that He is always with you. How can you use this reminder to face any fears you might have today?

PRAYER

Dear God, thank You for always being by my side, especially when I feel scared or unsure. Help me to remember Your strength and love, so I can face my fears with courage and joy each day.

ROOTED IN GOD'S WORD

"Let the word of Christ dwell in you richly." Colossians 3:16

DEVOTIONAL

God's Word is like a strong tree that gives us life. When we let the words of Jesus fill our hearts, we grow closer to Him. Think of reading the Bible as watering a plant; it helps us understand God's love and guidance. Each time we discover a new verse, we find strength and wisdom for our day. Let's make time to read the Bible daily, allowing it to grow deep roots in us, helping us bloom in faith.

DAILY REFLECTION

As you think about how God's Word is like a strong tree that gives us life, consider this: What is one verse or story from the Bible that has helped you feel closer to God? How can you make time to "water" that part of your faith this week?

PRAYER

Dear God, thank you for your Word, which is like a strong tree that gives us life and help us grow closer to You. Please help us to spend time in the Bible, discovering verses that fill our hearts with Your love and guidance, so we can bloom in faith every day.

FAITH FOR THE FUTURE

"For I know the plans I have for you," declares the Lord, "plans to prosper you and not to harm you, plans to give you hope and a future." Jeremiah 29:11

DEVOTIONAL

God has beautiful plans for each of us, even if we can't see them yet. In Jeremiah 29:11, He reminds us that His plans are good! When we trust in Him, we find hope for tomorrow. Sometimes, we feel scared or unsure about the future, but God is there to guide us. Whenever you feel worried, remember to pray and listen to Him. Trust that every day can be a step toward His wonderful dreams for you.

DAILY REFLECTION

Think about a time when you felt unsure about what was going to happen next in your life. How did you find comfort or hope in that moment? What steps can you take to trust God more as you look to the future?

PRAYER

Dear God, thank you for the beautiful plans you have for each of us that we may not yet see. When we feel scared or unsure, help us to trust in you and listen for your gentle guidance, knowing that each step we take can lead us closer to your wonderful dreams for our lives.

CHOOSING JOY DAILY

"This is the day that the Lord has made; let us rejoice and be glad in it." Psalm 118:24

DEVOTIONAL

Every day is a gift from God, filled with new opportunities to choose joy! Psalm 118:24 reminds us that today is special because the Lord made it just for us. When we wake up, let's take a moment to notice the little things that make us smile—the sun shining, a kind word from a friend, or even our favorite breakfast. By choosing to rejoice, we can fill our hearts with happiness and grow closer to God each day!

DAILY REFLECTION

Reflect on the little things in your life that bring you joy each day. What are three simple moments or discoveries that made you smile today? How can recognizing these moments help you feel more connected to God and grateful for the opportunities in each day?

PRAYER

Dear God, thank you for this beautiful day filled with new chances to find joy in the little things that surround us. Help us to see the brightness in each moment and feel your love guiding us as we celebrate the blessings of today.

GOD'S PRESENCE IN THE WAITING

"Be still, and know that I am God." Psalm 46:10

DEVOTIONAL

Sometimes, waiting can feel slow and hard. But God reminds us in Psalm 46:10 to "Be still, and know that I am God." When we pause and take a breath, we can feel His love and presence with us. In these quiet moments, we can pray, read His Word, or simply listen. Remember, God is always with you, even when it seems like nothing is happening. Trust Him, for He has wonderful plans for you, even in the waiting.

DAILY REFLECTION

When you find yourself waiting for something and it feels slow or hard, how can you take a moment to be still and remember that God is with you? What help do you think prayer or reading His Word could bring during those times?

PRAYER

Dear God, help me to be still and remember that You are always with me, even when I feel like nothing is happening. Teach me to pause, listen, and find comfort in Your love as I wait for the good things You have planned for me.

April 7

A HEART OF HUMILITY

"Humble yourselves before the Lord, and he will lift you up."
James 4:10

DEVOTIONAL

Humility means recognizing that we aren't perfect and that we need God's help. When we humble ourselves before the Lord, we show Him that we trust His plan for our lives. James 4:10 reminds us that when we do this, God lifts us up and gives us strength. Take a moment today to pray and ask God to help you be humble. Remember, it's in our humility that we grow closer to Him and truly find our worth.

DAILY REFLECTION

What is one area in your life where you can practice humility this week, and how can you ask God for help in that situation?

PRAYER

Dear God, help me to remember that I am not perfect and that I need Your guidance each day. Teach me to be humble in my heart, trusting in Your plan for my life, so that I can grow closer to You and feel the strength of Your love.

April 8

WALKING IN GOD'S STRENGTH

"I can do all things through Christ who strengthens me."
Philippians 4:13

DEVOTIONAL

When we feel tired or scared, it can be hard to keep going. But there's good news! Philippians 4:13 reminds us that we can do anything when we trust in Jesus. He gives us strength when we need it most. When facing challenges, remember: you are never alone! Talk to God in prayer, and ask for His help. As you walk in His strength, you'll discover that you can do amazing things with His love guiding you.

DAILY REFLECTION

When you feel tired or scared, how can you remind yourself that you are never alone and that God is there to give you strength? Think of a recent challenge you faced—how did you talk to God about it, and what amazing things did you discover as you walked in His love?

PRAYER

Dear God, when I feel tired or scared, help me to remember that You are always with me, giving me strength and courage. Thank You for loving me and showing me that I can do amazing things when I trust in You.

COMPASSION LIKE CHRIST

"Be compassionate, just as your Father is compassionate." Luke 6:36

DEVOTIONAL

Today, let's remember to show compassion, just like Jesus! In Luke 6:36, we learn that God is always kind and caring. When we see someone sad or in need, we have a chance to be like Him. Compassion means helping others, listening to them, and sharing a smile. It's simple but very important. When we practice compassion, we grow closer to God and show His love to the world. Let's be His hands and heart today!

DAILY REFLECTION

How can you look for opportunities in your day to show kindness and compassion to someone who might be feeling sad or in need?

PRAYER

Dear God, thank You for teaching us to be kind and compassionate, just like Jesus. Help us to open our hearts and look for moments today when we can share Your love by helping others and bringing smiles to those who need them.

OVERCOMING SPIRITUAL BURNOUT

"But those who hope in the Lord will renew their strength. They will soar on wings like eagles; they will run and not grow weary, they will walk and not be faint." Isaiah 40:31

DEVOTIONAL

Feeling tired or worn out in your spiritual life is normal. Isaiah 40:31 reminds us that when we place our hopes in the Lord, He gives us new strength. Imagine soaring like an eagle—strong and free! When we spend time in prayer or read the Bible, we fill our hearts with God's love and power. So, if you're feeling heavy, take a moment to pause, reflect, and let God renew your spirit. He promises to lift you up!

DAILY REFLECTION

How can you intentionally create space in your day to connect with God and recharge your spirit, especially when you're feeling tired or worn out?

PRAYER

Dear God, when I feel tired and worn out, help me to pause and seek Your presence, knowing that You renew my spirit like the soaring eagle. Thank You for Your promise to lift me up and fill my heart with Your love and strength.

THE HOPE OF THE RESURRECTION

"For I know that my Redeemer lives, and that in the end He will stand on the earth." Job 19:25

DEVOTIONAL

In tough times, remember Job's words: "For I know that my Redeemer lives." Job faced many struggles, but he held onto hope in God. Just like Job, we can trust that Jesus is alive and will stand with us, no matter what challenges we face. His resurrection teaches us that, even when things seem dark, there is always hope for a new beginning. Let this promise strengthen your faith and inspire you to trust in God's love each day.

DAILY REFLECTION

How can you apply Job's words, "For I know that my Redeemer lives," to your own life during difficult times? Consider a challenge you are currently facing and think about how trusting in God's love and the hope of new beginnings can help you through it.

PRAYER

Dear God, even when times are tough and we feel uncertain, help us to remember that You are always with us, just like You were with Job. May we find comfort in knowing that our Redeemer lives, filling our hearts with hope and strength to face each challenge we encounter.

POURING OUT, BEING FILLED

"But he said, 'I will pour out my Spirit on all people.'" Acts 2:17

DEVOTIONAL

God wants to fill our hearts with His Spirit! In Acts 2:17, He promises to pour out His Spirit on everyone. Imagine a cup being filled to the brim— this is how God wants to fill us with love, joy, and guidance. When we open our hearts and share kindness and joy with others, we make room for even more of God in our lives. Let's ask God to fill us up today, so we can pour out His goodness to the world!

DAILY REFLECTION

How can you open your heart today to receive God's Spirit and share His love and joy with someone around you?

PRAYER

Dear God, thank you for wanting to fill our hearts with Your Spirit, just like a cup overflowing with love and joy. Help us to open our hearts wide today so we can receive Your goodness and share it with everyone around us.

GOD'S PROVISION IS ENOUGH

"And my God will supply every need of yours according to his riches in glory in Christ Jesus." Philippians 4:19

DEVOTIONAL

God loves you and wants to take care of you! Philippians 4:19 reminds us that He will provide everything we truly need. Sometimes we may worry about not having enough, but God sees our hearts and knows what we require. Trust in Him! Each day, thank God for what you have and ask Him to help you see His blessings. Remember, His love is richer than anything else, and with Him, you will always have enough.

DAILY REFLECTION

As you think about the ways God provides for you, what are three things you can be thankful for today that show His love and care in your life? How can you remember these blessings when you start to feel worried about having enough?

PRAYER

Dear God, thank You for loving me so much and always taking care of my needs. Help me to remember the blessings You give each day, and may I trust in Your rich love to ease my worries and fill my heart with gratitude.

WOMEN OF PURPOSE

"She is clothed with strength and dignity; she can laugh at the days to come." Proverbs 31:25

DEVOTIONAL

Today, let's celebrate the strength and dignity of women. Proverbs 31:25 tells us that a woman of purpose can face the future with joy. This means trusting God, no matter what challenges come her way. When we walk with Him, we find the courage to smile, even when life is tough. Each day, let's remember to be strong like the women in the Bible, finding joy in every moment as we follow God's path for us.

DAILY REFLECTION

How can you embrace the strength and dignity within yourself today, and what steps can you take to trust God in facing any challenges that may come your way?

PRAYER

Dear God, thank you for the strong and wonderful women in our lives who inspire us to face challenges with courage and joy. Help us to embrace our own strength and dignity, trusting in You each day as we walk along the path You have laid out for us.

COURAGE TO BEGIN AGAIN

"Be strong and courageous; do not be afraid; do not be discouraged, for the Lord your God will be with you wherever you go." Joshua 1:9

DEVOTIONAL

Sometimes we feel stuck or afraid to start over. But God wants us to be strong and brave! In Joshua 1:9, God tells us not to be afraid because He is always with us. When we face new challenges or need to try again, remember that God walks beside us, helping us grow and learn. Take a deep breath, pray for courage, and step forward. Every new beginning is a chance to build a stronger faith.

DAILY REFLECTION

Reflect on a time when you felt stuck or afraid to try something new. How did you find the courage to take a step forward, and how did you sense God's presence with you during that experience? What lessons from that moment can you apply to future challenges you may face?

PRAYER

Dear God, when I feel stuck or afraid to try again, remind me that You are always by my side, giving me the courage to step forward with strength and bravery. Help me to embrace new beginnings as opportunities to grow in faith and trust in Your loving presence guiding my way.

FAITHFUL IN THE HIDDEN PLACES

"Whatever you do, work heartily, as for the Lord and not for men." Colossians 3:23

DEVOTIONAL

In everyday tasks, like cleaning your room or helping a friend, remember that God sees all you do, even when no one else does. Colossians 3:23 reminds us to work with our whole heart, as if we are doing it for God. When you choose to be faithful in the hidden places, you grow closer to Him. Trust that your small efforts matter and build a strong connection with God. Every act of kindness is a step in your faith journey.

DAILY REFLECTION

As you think about your everyday tasks, how can you remind yourself that even small acts, like cleaning your room or helping a friend, are important in your journey of faith? What are some ways you can approach these tasks with your whole heart, knowing that God sees your efforts?

PRAYER

Dear God, thank you for seeing the little things I do, like cleaning my room and being kind to my friends; help me to remember that every small effort counts in my journey with You. Please fill my heart with joy as I work with all my strength, knowing that I am doing it for You and drawing closer to Your love.

LIVING LIGHT IN A HEAVY WORLD

"You are the light of the world. A city set on a hill cannot be hidden." Matthew 5:14

DEVOTIONAL

In a world that can feel dark and heavy, remember that you are called to shine brightly! Jesus says you are the light of the world. Just like a shining city on a hill, your love and kindness can guide others. When you share joy, help a friend, or show forgiveness, you reveal God's light. Today, let your actions reflect His love. Each small act makes a big difference, showing everyone around you the beauty of living in faith.

DAILY REFLECTION

How can you share a little bit of God's light with someone today through your actions or words? Think of one specific way you can show kindness, joy, or forgiveness to someone around you.

PRAYER

Dear God, thank You for reminding me that I can shine brightly in this world with my love and kindness. Help me to share Your light today by being a friend to someone in need or showing forgiveness, so that others may feel Your warmth through my actions.

TRUSTING GOD WITH THE UNKNOWN

"Trust in the Lord with all your heart and lean not on your own understanding." Proverbs 3:5

DEVOTIONAL

In life, we often face things we don't understand. Sometimes, it feels scary not knowing what comes next. Proverbs 3:5 reminds us to trust God with our whole heart. This means believing that He has a good plan for us, even when we can't see it. Think of it like a treasure map! We might not know the path, but God does. Let's pray and ask Him to help us trust Him more each day.

DAILY REFLECTION

How can you trust God more in your life when you encounter things that are confusing or scary? Think of a time when you didn't know what would happen next. How did it make you feel, and how can you remember to trust God's plan in those moments?

PRAYER

Dear God, even when we feel scared or confused, help us to trust You with our whole hearts, just like a treasure map leading us to Your wonderful plan. Remind us in those uncertain moments that You are always there, guiding us and knowing what's best for us.

EMBRACING GOD'S REFINING

"For I know the plans I have for you, declares the Lord, plans to prosper you and not to harm you, plans to give you hope and a future." Jeremiah 29:11

DEVOTIONAL

God has a special plan just for you, filled with good things that help you grow. Sometimes, life feels tough, but remember that God is like a gardener, lovingly shaping and refining you. Just as precious metals are made shiny through fire, God uses challenges to make you stronger. Trust His plans, for they are full of hope and promise. Whenever you feel uncertain, remember that God is always guiding you toward a wonderful future.

DAILY REFLECTION

When you feel spiritually empty, how can you remind yourself of the good things God has planned for you, even in tough times?

PRAYER

Dear God, thank you for your special plan filled with good things just for me. Help me to trust in your love, even when times are tough, and remind me that you are always guiding me toward a bright and beautiful future.

GRATITUDE IN THE GRIND

"Rejoice always, pray continually, give thanks in all circumstances; for this is God's will for you in Christ Jesus." 1 Thessalonians 5:16-18

DEVOTIONAL

Life can be challenging, and days can feel heavy. Yet, in every moment, God invites us to rejoice! 1 Thessalonians 5:16-18 reminds us to always celebrate the good, pray as we navigate the tough times, and give thanks for every experience. Even when things are hard, there's something to be grateful for—a lesson learned, a friend's support, or a moment of peace. Let's practice gratitude in our daily grind, trusting that God is with us through it all.

DAILY REFLECTION

Reflect on a challenging moment you faced recently. What specific lesson did you learn from that experience, and how can you express gratitude for the support or peace you found during that time?

PRAYER

Dear God, thank you for being with us in every moment, for reminding us that even on tough days, there is always something to celebrate and learn from. Help us to open our hearts to gratitude, recognizing the support of friends and the peace that comes from knowing you are by our side.

HOLDING ON TO HOPE

"For I know the plans I have for you, declares the Lord, plans to prosper you and not to harm you, plans to give you hope and a future." Jeremiah 29:11

DEVOTIONAL

God has wonderful plans just for you! Sometimes, life can feel tough, and it's easy to lose hope. But remember, God promises us a bright future filled with peace and love. When you feel uncertain or scared, hold on to the truth that He is always working for your good. Pray and trust that everything will turn out okay, because He loves you and wants the best for you. Keep your heart hopeful; God is guiding every step you take.

DAILY REFLECTION

What is one thing you can do this week to remind yourself that God has a special plan for you, even when things feel tough?

PRAYER

Dear God, thank you for the wonderful plans you have just for me. Help me to trust in your love and guidance, especially when life feels tough, so I can always remember that brighter days are ahead.

This week, try writing down one thing you love about yourself or one thing you are thankful for to remind yourself of the special plans God has for you.

GOD'S STILL SMALL VOICE

"And after the fire came a gentle whisper." 1 Kings 19:12

DEVOTIONAL

Sometimes, God speaks in a quiet whisper, not loud storms or big fires. In 1 Kings 19:12, we learn that after the noise, God's gentle voice came to Elijah. This teaches us to listen closely. In our busy lives, it's easy to miss His words. Take a moment each day to be still —close your eyes, breathe deeply, and open your heart. God wants to guide you and share His love through that gentle whisper.

DAILY REFLECTION

Reflect on a time when you felt overwhelmed by noise and distractions in your life. How can you create a quiet space each day to listen for God's gentle whisper? What might you be missing if you don't take the time to be still and open your heart to Him?

PRAYER

Dear God, help us to find moments of stillness in our busy days, so we can hear Your gentle whispers of love and guidance. Open our hearts to feel Your presence, reminding us that even in the noise, Your quiet voice is always there, waiting for us to listen.

THE BEAUTY OF FORGIVENESS

"For if you forgive other people when they sin against you, your heavenly Father will also forgive you." Matthew 6:14

DEVOTIONAL

Forgiveness is like a gift we give ourselves and others. When someone hurts us, it can feel heavy in our hearts. But God teaches us that by forgiving them, we can let go of that weight. Jesus reminds us in Matthew 6:14 that when we forgive others, we open our hearts to receive God's love and forgiveness too. Let's practice forgiving each day, just as God forgives us. It helps us grow closer to Him and brings peace to our hearts.

DAILY REFLECTION

Think about a time when someone hurt you and it felt heavy in your heart. How could forgiving that person help you feel lighter and open your heart more to God's love? What is one small step you can take today towards forgiveness?

PRAYER

Dear God, help us to remember that forgiveness is a beautiful gift we can give ourselves and others, lightening our hearts and drawing us closer to Your love. Teach us to let go of our hurts, just as You forgive us, so we may feel the peace and joy that comes from sharing Your kindness with the world.

WHEN YOU FEEL SPIRITUALLY EMPTY

"Come to me, all you who are weary and burdened, and I will give you rest." Matthew 11:28

DEVOTIONAL

Sometimes, we feel tired and empty inside, like our joy has run out. Jesus invites us, "Come to me, all you who are weary and burdened, and I will give you rest." When you feel this way, remember that you can talk to God anytime. He loves to hear your thoughts and feelings. Spend a moment in prayer or read your Bible. He will fill your heart with peace and strength, helping you grow closer to Him.

DAILY REFLECTION

When you feel tired or empty inside, how can you remind yourself to turn to God in those moments? What are some ways you can share your feelings with Him through prayer or reading the Bible?

PRAYER

Dear God, when I feel tired or empty inside, help me remember that I can always come to You for comfort and strength. Thank You for listening to my thoughts and feelings, and for filling my heart with Your love.

PEACE THAT TRANSCENDS

"And the peace of God, which surpasses all understanding, will guard your hearts and your minds in Christ Jesus." Philippians 4:7

DEVOTIONAL

Life can sometimes feel like a storm, but God's peace is like a gentle shelter amidst chaos. Philippians 4:7 tells us that God's peace is beyond what we can imagine. When we trust Him with our worries, He helps calm our hearts and minds. Take a moment today to pray and share your concerns with God. Allow His peace to fill you and guard you, helping you feel secure and loved no matter what you face.

DAILY REFLECTION

Reflect on a time when you felt overwhelmed or anxious, like you were in the midst of a storm. How did you turn to God during that moment, and what did you experience as you surrendered your worries to Him? What is one way you can invite God's peace into your heart today?

PRAYER

Dear God, when life's storms feel overwhelming, help me to find comfort in Your peace, knowing that You are my gentle shelter. I trust You with my worries and invite Your calming presence into my heart, reminding me that I am always loved and safe in Your care.

CARRYING GOD'S LIGHT

"Let your light shine before others, that they may see your good deeds and glorify your Father in heaven." Matthew 5:16

DEVOTIONAL

Each of us has a special light inside, a gift from God. When we do kind things for others, like sharing and helping, we let that light shine bright! Think about how happy it makes you when someone smiles because of your actions. Remember, when we share our love and kindness, people can see God's goodness through us. Today, let's look for ways to shine our light, so others can feel God's love and praise Him!

DAILY REFLECTION

How can you let your special light shine today by showing kindness to someone else? Think of one small thing you can do that might make someone smile.

PRAYER

Dear God, thank you for the special light within each of us that shines brightly when we show kindness and love. Help us to find little ways to share our light today, so others can feel your goodness and joy through our actions.

April 27

STANDING ON GOD'S PROMISES

"For all the promises of God find their Yes in him." 2 Corinthians 1:20

DEVOTIONAL

Every promise God makes is true and can be trusted! In 2 Corinthians 1:20, we learn that all of God's promises are fulfilled in Jesus. This means you can always rely on Him for help, comfort, and love. When life gets tough or scary, remember that God is with you and keeps His word. Pray, read the Bible, and trust Him daily. Standing on God's promises gives you strength and joy, no matter what happens!

DAILY REFLECTION

Reflect on a time when you felt scared or uncertain. How did remembering God's promises help you through that situation? Write down one specific promise from the Bible that gives you strength, and consider how you can remind yourself of this promise in your daily life.

PRAYER

Dear God, thank you for always keeping your promises and for being our safe place when life feels tough or uncertain. Help us to remember that you are with us, filling our hearts with love and strength as we trust in your words each day.

April 28

FINDING REST IN HIS LOVE

"Come to me, all who labor and are heavy laden, and I will give you rest." Matthew 11:28

DEVOTIONAL

When you feel tired or worried, remember that Jesus invites you to come to Him. He loves you and wants to take away your heavy burdens. Just as a cozy blanket brings warmth, His love wraps around you, bringing peace. Take a moment to talk to Him in prayer. Share your worries and ask for rest. God promises to help and comfort you. Trust in His love, and you will find true rest for your heart.

DAILY REFLECTION

When you're feeling tired or worried, how can you remind yourself to talk to Jesus and share your feelings with Him? What does it feel like to trust in His love and find rest for your heart?

PRAYER

Dear Jesus, when I start to feel tired or worried, help me remember to come to You and share my feelings. Wrap me in Your loving comfort, so I can trust in Your peace and find rest for my heart.

WALKING BY FAITH, NOT SIGHT

"For we walk by faith, not by sight." 2 Corinthians 5:7

DEVOTIONAL

Walking by faith means trusting God even when we can't see the whole path ahead. Just like a child holding a parent's hand, we can take steps forward, knowing God is guiding us. Sometimes, things may look scary or confusing, but faith helps us to believe that He has a good plan for us. Each time we trust Him, we grow stronger. Today, remember to take a step in faith, believing God is with you every step of the way.

DAILY REFLECTION

As you reflect on your journey of faith, think about a time when you felt uncertain or afraid about what was ahead. How did trusting God in that moment help you take a step forward? What is one small step you can take today to strengthen your faith and trust in His guidance?

PRAYER

Dear God, thank you for being with me and guiding me as I walk on this journey of faith. Help me to trust you when things seem confusing or scary, and remind me that each small step I take in faith brings me closer to your loving plan for my life.

GOD'S GRACE THROUGH EVERY SEASON

"My grace is sufficient for you, for my power is made perfect in weakness." 2 Corinthians 12:9

DEVOTIONAL

God's grace is like a warm blanket that covers us in every season of life. When we feel weak or unsure, remember that God's strength shines through us. Just like a flower grows through rain and sunshine, we can grow in our faith during tough times. Trust that God's grace is always enough, making us stronger and bringing us peace. Let's keep our hearts open to His love, knowing He is with us in every moment.

DAILY REFLECTION

How have you experienced God's grace in both the challenging and joyful moments of your life, and how can you lean on that grace to grow in your faith during uncertain times?

PRAYER

Dear God, thank You for Your grace that wraps around us like a warm blanket, helping us feel Your love in every season of our lives. Please help us to remember that even in difficult times, Your strength shines through us, guiding our hearts to trust in You and grow in faith.

GRACE FOR TODAY

"But he said to me, 'My grace is sufficient for you, for my power is made perfect in weakness.'" 2 Corinthians 12:9

DEVOTIONAL

Every day can bring challenges that make us feel weak or unsure. But remember, God tells us, "My grace is enough for you." This means that even when things feel tough, God's love and strength will help us through. When we trust Him, His power shines in our weaknesses. Let's stop trying to be perfect and instead lean into God's grace. Today, take a moment to thank God for giving you the strength you need!

DAILY REFLECTION

Reflect on a time when you faced a challenge that made you feel weak or unsure. How did you see God's grace helping you through that situation? Take a moment to write down or share what you are thankful for today regarding God's support in your life.

PRAYER

Dear God, thank you for your amazing grace that helps me when I feel weak or unsure. I trust in Your love to guide me through each challenge, knowing I am never alone.

BECOMING A PRAYERFUL WOMAN

"Devote yourselves to prayer, being watchful and thankful." Colossians 4:2

DEVOTIONAL

Being a prayerful woman means talking to God every day and sharing our joys, worries, and thanks. Colossians 4:2 reminds us to devote ourselves to prayer, staying watchful and thankful. This means we should listen carefully for God's guidance and always remember to say thank you for the little things. As we pray, our hearts grow closer to God, and we discover His peace and love, helping us to shine brightly in the world around us.

DAILY REFLECTION

How can you practice being grateful today, and what are some things you can talk to God about that will help you feel closer to Him?

PRAYER

Dear God, thank you for this day and all the small blessings that fill it; help me to share my joys and worries with you, knowing you are always there to listen. As I talk to you, guide my heart to feel your peace and love, so that I can shine brightly and spread kindness to those around me.

GOD'S STRENGTH IN YOUR STORY

"I can do all things through Christ who strengthens me." Philippians 4:13

DEVOTIONAL

Every story has challenges, and sometimes we feel weak or unsure. In Philippians 4:13, we learn that we can do all things through Christ who gives us strength. When you face hard times, remember that you are not alone. Jesus is with you, helping you to be brave and strong. Trust in Him, and you'll find the energy to keep going. God is writing your story, and with His strength, you can overcome anything!

DAILY REFLECTION

Think about a time when you faced a challenge that made you feel weak or unsure. How did you remember that Jesus was with you during that time? What helped you to stay strong and keep going?

PRAYER

Dear God, thank you for being with us when we face challenges and for giving us the strength to keep going. Help us to trust in Your love and remember that with You by our side, we can be brave and overcome anything.

RESTORING YOUR SOUL

"He restores my soul; He guides me in paths of righteousness for His name's sake." Psalm 23:3

DEVOTIONAL

God loves you and knows when you feel tired or lost. In Psalm 23:3, we learn that He restores our souls. Imagine a cozy blanket wrapped around you, bringing comfort and warmth. When you pray or read the Bible, God helps heal your worries and shows you the right path to follow. Trust Him to guide you every day. By spending time with Him, you'll feel refreshed and ready to share His love with others.

DAILY REFLECTION

When you think about times when you feel tired or a little lost, how does knowing that God loves you and wants to help you feel like a warm blanket around you? What is one way you can spend a little time with God today to feel more comforted and refreshed?

PRAYER

Dear God, thank you for your unwavering love that comforts us like a warm blanket when we feel tired or lost. Please guide us on our paths and help us to take a moment today to spend time with you, so we can feel refreshed and ready to share your love with others.

TRUSTING GOD IN THE UNKNOWN

"Trust in the Lord with all your heart and lean not on your own understanding." Proverbs 3:5

DEVOTIONAL

In life, we often face things we don't understand, like the future or big changes. Proverbs 3:5 reminds us to trust in God with all our hearts. This means believing that He has a good plan for us, even when things seem scary or unclear. When we lean on our own understanding, we might feel lost. But when we trust God's love and wisdom, we find comfort and peace, knowing He is always with us.

DAILY REFLECTION

How can you remind yourself to trust God's plan when you face something that feels uncertain or scary in your life?

PRAYER

Dear God, when I feel unsure or scared about what lies ahead, help me to remember to trust in You with all my heart. Thank You for your loving plan; please fill me with peace as I lean on Your wisdom and know You are always by my side.

OVERFLOWING WITH COMPASSION

"Be compassionate as your Father is compassionate." Luke 6:36

DEVOTIONAL

Compassion is like a warm hug for the heart. When we show kindness and understanding to others, we reflect the love of our Father in heaven. Just as God cares for us, we are called to care for those around us. This week, look for ways to be compassionate—whether it's sharing a smile, lending a hand, or listening to a friend. Each small act can brighten someone's day and bring us closer to God's heart.

DAILY REFLECTION

Reflect on a time when you felt the warmth of someone's kindness. How did it make you feel, and how did it impact your day? Now think about ways you can offer that same warmth to someone else this week. What small acts of compassion can you commit to?

PRAYER

Dear God, thank you for the warmth of Your love, which teaches us to be kind and caring towards others. Help us to share that love through small acts of compassion, so we can brighten the hearts of those around us just as You brighten our days.

THE POWER OF A GRATEFUL HEART

"Give thanks in all circumstances; for this is the will of God in Christ Jesus for you." 1 Thessalonians 5:18

DEVOTIONAL

Being grateful is like wearing special glasses that help us see the good in everything, even when times are tough. In 1 Thessalonians 5:18, God tells us to "give thanks in all circumstances." This means we should look for things to be thankful for every day, no matter how we feel. When we practice gratitude, our hearts grow closer to God, and we find joy in even the smallest blessings. Let's try to thank God for His goodness today!

DAILY REFLECTION

As you look at your day today, what is one small thing you can find to be grateful for, even if it might feel challenging right now? How does recognizing that blessing change your perspective?

PRAYER

Dear God, thank you for the special gift of gratitude that helps us see the good in every moment, even when things feel hard. Please help us to always find something to be thankful for, so our hearts can grow closer to You and fill our days with joy.

FAITH IN THE STORM

"For I know the plans I have for you, declares the Lord, plans to prosper you and not to harm you, plans to give you hope and a future." Jeremiah 29:11

DEVOTIONAL

When storms come into our lives, it can feel scary and overwhelming. But remember, God has a wonderful plan just for you! In Jeremiah 29:11, He tells us that His plans are filled with hope and goodness. Even when things seem tough, trust that God is with you, guiding you through each wave. Keep your eyes on Him, and you will find peace. Every storm will help you grow closer to Him and strengthen your faith.

DAILY REFLECTION

Reflect on a time when you faced a difficult situation that felt like a storm in your life. How did you see God guiding you through that experience, and what did you learn about His plans for you during that time?

PRAYER

Dear God, when storms come into our lives and things feel scary, help us to trust in Your wonderful plan for us, knowing that You are always guiding our way. Help us to keep our eyes on You, so we can find peace and grow closer to Your loving heart, even in the toughest times. Amen.

WHEN YOU FEEL INVISIBLE

"But even the hairs of your head are all numbered. Fear not; you are of more value than many sparrows." Luke 12:7

DEVOTIONAL

Sometimes, we might feel invisible, like no one notices us. But remember, God sees you and loves you deeply. Jesus said that even the hairs on your head are counted! This means you are incredibly valuable to Him. When you feel alone or unnoticed, talk to God. Share your feelings and let Him remind you of your worth. You are important and loved, just like every sparrow in the sky. Trust in His care and never forget you matter.

DAILY REFLECTION

Think about a time when you felt unnoticed or invisible. How can you remind yourself that God sees you, loves you, and cares for you in that moment? Share your feelings with God and write down what makes you feel valued and important.

PRAYER

Dear God, thank you for always seeing me and loving me, even when I feel invisible. Help me remember that I am valuable and cherished, just like every beautiful sparrow you created, and that I can always talk to you about my feelings.

May 10

ROOTED IN GOD'S LOVE

"For I am convinced that neither death nor life, neither angels nor demons, neither the present nor the future, nor any powers, will be able to separate us from the love of God that is in Christ Jesus our Lord." Romans 8:38-39

DEVOTIONAL

God loves you more than you can imagine! Romans 8:38-39 reminds us that nothing can ever take that love away. Whether you're feeling happy, sad, or confused, God is always there, holding you close. Think of a strong tree with deep roots; just like that tree, you can grow tall and strong in God's love. Whenever you feel unsure, remember that His love is always with you, no matter what. Trust Him, and you will flourish!

DAILY REFLECTION

How can you remind yourself of God's unconditional love when you're feeling down or unsure, just like the strong tree that grows deep roots?

PRAYER

Dear God, thank you for your amazing love that never goes away, even when I feel sad or confused. Help me remember that I can grow strong like a tree because your love is always holding me close, no matter what I'm feeling.

A QUIET SPIRIT, A POWERFUL FAITH

"For we live by faith, not by sight." 2 Corinthians 5:7

DEVOTIONAL

In our busy lives, it's easy to get distracted by what we see around us. But God asks us to live by faith, trusting in His promises even when things seem uncertain. A quiet spirit helps us listen to His voice and grow stronger in our faith. When we focus on God and believe in His goodness, we can find peace and strength. Remember, true power comes not from what we see, but from trusting in God's love every day.

DAILY REFLECTION

As you reflect on your day, consider this question: In what ways have you noticed distractions pulling you away from trusting in God's promises? How can you create moments of quiet in your day to focus on His voice and experience His peace?

PRAYER

Dear God, help us to quiet our hearts and listen for Your gentle voice amidst the distractions of our busy days. Teach us to trust in Your promises, so we may find peace and strength in Your love, no matter what life brings our way.

MOTHERING WITH GRACE

"Her children rise up and call her blessed." Proverbs 31:28

DEVOTIONAL

Mothering with grace means loving our children patiently and teaching them about God. When we care for them, help them grow, and share kind words, they see God's love through us. Proverbs 31:28 tells us that children will honor their mothers when they feel this love. Let's pray for wisdom and strength to guide our families with grace. By showing love, we not only bless our children but also show them how to bless others.

DAILY REFLECTION

How can you show love and patience to your children today, and in what ways can you help them learn about God's love through your actions and words?

PRAYER

Dear God, please grant us the wisdom and strength to nurture our children with gentle love and kindness, reflecting Your grace in our actions and words. Help us to teach them about Your love so they may grow to honor and bless others as they feel our love in their hearts.

PERSEVERING IN PRAYER

"Pray without ceasing." 1 Thessalonians 5:17

DEVOTIONAL

Prayer is like a special chat with God. In 1 Thessalonians 5:17, we're reminded to "pray without ceasing." This means we can talk to God anytime—whether we're happy, sad, or confused. Just like a friend doesn't stop talking to you, God loves to hear from you always. Even if it feels hard sometimes, keep praying. Your heart grows closer to Him, and He will guide you every step of the way. Remember, God is always listening!

DAILY REFLECTION

How can you make time to talk to God in your daily life, and what are some things you want to share with Him during your conversations?

PRAYER

Dear God, thank you for being my best friend who loves to listen whenever I need to talk. Help me to remember to share my thoughts and feelings with you every day, knowing you are always there to guide me and keep my heart close to yours.

THE LORD IS YOUR SHEPHERD

"The Lord is my shepherd; I shall not want." Psalm 23:1

DEVOTIONAL

The Lord is our Shepherd, which means He cares for us like a loving guide. Just as a shepherd watches over sheep, God watches over us, providing everything we need. When we trust Him, we don't have to worry about what tomorrow brings. We can find comfort in knowing that He leads us to peaceful places and helps us through hard times. Remember, God loves you so much and is always by your side, ready to guide you.

DAILY REFLECTION

How can you remind yourself that God is always watching over you, especially during times when you feel worried or uncertain?

PRAYER

Dear God, thank you for being our loving Shepherd who cares for us and guides us through every moment. Help us to remember that you are always with us, bringing peace to our hearts and comfort in our worries.

LETTING GO OF BITTERNESS

"Get rid of all bitterness, rage and anger, brawling and slander, along with every form of malice." Ephesians 4:31

DEVOTIONAL

Bitterness can weigh us down, like carrying a heavy backpack that slows us down. In Ephesians 4:31, God tells us to let go of anger and hurt. When we release these feelings, we make space for love and joy to fill our hearts. Imagine how freeing it feels to forgive others and move on! Today, take a moment to pray and ask God to help you let go of any bitterness. Trust Him to guide you toward peace and happiness.

DAILY REFLECTION

What is one situation or person in your life that you feel you need to forgive in order to let go of bitterness and create space for love and joy? Take a moment to think about how you can begin to release those feelings and what positive change you hope to experience in your heart.

PRAYER

Dear God, please help me to let go of any bitterness I might be holding onto, so my heart can be filled with love and joy. Guide me to forgive those who have hurt me, so I can find peace and share kindness with others.

WALKING IN SPIRITUAL FREEDOM

"It is for freedom that Christ has set us free; stand firm, then, and do not let yourselves be burdened again by a yoke of slavery." Galatians 5:1

DEVOTIONAL

Jesus wants us to live freely, just like a bird soaring in the sky. Galatians 5:1 reminds us that Christ has set us free from worry, fear, and bad choices. When we trust in Him, we can let go of anything that weighs us down. Remember, standing firm in this freedom means choosing joy and love every day. Let go of anything that chains you, and embrace the wonderful life God has for you!

DAILY REFLECTION

As you think about how Jesus wants you to live freely, what are some worries or fears in your life that you can let go of today? How can you choose joy and love in these situations instead?

PRAYER

Dear Jesus, thank you for setting us free to live joyfully like birds soaring in the sky, away from worries and fears that hold us back. Help us remember to choose love and happiness every day, trusting in Your goodness to let go of anything that keeps us from the beautiful life You have for us.

YOUR STORY ISN'T OVER

"For I know the plans I have for you, declares the Lord, plans to prosper you and not to harm you, plans to give you hope and a future." Jeremiah 29:11

DEVOTIONAL

Your story isn't over! God has amazing plans just for you. Sometimes, things might feel hard or confusing, but remember what God says in Jeremiah 29:11. He has plans to help you grow, to give you hope, and to lead you to a bright future. No matter where you are in life, trust that God is writing your story. Stay close to Him, and you'll see how beautiful your journey can be. Keep believing!

DAILY REFLECTION

Reflect on a time when you felt confused or uncertain about your future. How did you feel in that moment, and what did you do to find hope? How can you remind yourself that God is still writing your story, even during challenging times?

PRAYER

Dear God, thank You for reminding me that my story isn't finished and that You have wonderful plans just for me. Help me to trust in Your guidance during confusing times and to find comfort in knowing that You are always by my side, weaving my journey with love and hope.

STRENGTH TO FORGIVE

"For if you forgive other people when they sin against you, your heavenly Father will also forgive you." Matthew 6:14

DEVOTIONAL

Forgiving others can be hard, especially when we're hurt. But Jesus reminds us in Matthew 6:14 that forgiveness is important. When we let go of anger, we open our hearts to love and peace. Just as God forgives us, He wants us to show that same kindness to others. Ask God for strength to forgive those who've wronged you. Each time you forgive, you grow closer to Him and experience the joy of His love in your life.

DAILY REFLECTION

Think about a time when someone hurt you. How did it make you feel? Now, can you imagine what it would be like to let go of that hurt and choose to forgive? What steps can you take today to show kindness to that person, remembering that forgiveness can bring you closer to God's love and peace?

PRAYER

Dear God, help me to find the strength to forgive those who have hurt me, just as You forgive me. Teach me to let go of my anger, so I can open my heart to love and feel the joy of Your peace in my life.

FAITHFUL THROUGH THE SEASONS

"For I know the plans I have for you, declares the Lord, plans to prosper you and not to harm you, plans to give you hope and a future." Jeremiah 29:11

DEVOTIONAL

As the seasons change, remember that God remains the same. In Jeremiah 29:11, He promises us hope and a bright future. Just like trees grow stronger through winter's chill and summer's warmth, our faith deepens through life's ups and downs. Trust in God's plans, even when things seem uncertain. He knows what is best for you, guiding you with love. Embrace each season with faith, knowing that God is nurturing your heart every step of the way.

DAILY REFLECTION

As you think about the changing seasons in your life, what are some small victories you can celebrate that show how God has been guiding you through both challenging and joyful times?

PRAYER

Dear God, thank you for being a constant source of love and strength as the seasons of our lives change. Help us to celebrate the small victories that remind us of Your guiding hand, nurturing our hearts through every challenge and joy.

CHOSEN AND CHERISHED

"You are a chosen people, a royal priesthood, a holy nation, God's special possession." 1 Peter 2:9

DEVOTIONAL

You are special to God! In 1 Peter 2:9, we learn that we are chosen, just like a favorite toy or book. God sees us as precious and treats us with love. Remember, being part of His royal family means we can spread kindness and share His love with others. Each day, thank God for making you one of His chosen people. Trust that He always cherishes you, no matter what. You are loved just as you are!

DAILY REFLECTION

How can you show kindness to someone today, remembering that you are special to God and part of His royal family?

PRAYER

Dear God, thank You for making me special and part of Your royal family; help me to remember that I am loved just as I am. Please guide me to show kindness to others today, sharing Your love and light with everyone I meet.

GOD'S PEACE IN PRESSURE

"Do not be anxious about anything, but in every situation, by prayer and petition, with thanksgiving, present your requests to God. And the peace of God, which transcends all understanding, will guard your hearts and your minds in Christ Jesus." Philippians 4:6-7

DEVOTIONAL

When life feels heavy and you're worried, remember that God wants to help you. In Philippians 4:6-7, we learn to bring our worries to Him through prayer. Talk to God about what's troubling you, and thank Him for all the good things in your life. When you do this, His peace—like a warm blanket—will wrap around your heart and mind. Trust that God is with you, calming your fears and guiding your steps every day.

DAILY REFLECTION

What are some worries or heavy feelings you have right now, and how can you talk to God about them while also remembering to thank Him for the good things in your life?

PRAYER

Dear God, when I feel heavy with worries, I know You are here to help me, and I thank You for the good things in my life that bring me joy. Please wrap me in Your peace and comfort, guiding my heart and mind as I share my troubles with You.

A LIFE THAT BEARS FRUIT

"By this My Father is glorified, that you bear much fruit; so you will be My disciples." John 15:8

DEVOTIONAL

In John 15:8, Jesus teaches us that God is glorified when we bear fruit. Just like a tree that grows delicious apples, our lives can show love, kindness, and joy. To bear fruit, we need to stay close to Jesus, just like branches stay connected to a tree. Each day, ask God how you can share His love with others. When we live this way, we grow as His disciples and help others see His goodness through us.

DAILY REFLECTION

How can you take a moment today to show love or kindness to someone in your life, and how do you think that action might help others see God's goodness?

PRAYER

Dear God, help me stay close to Jesus so I can share Your love and kindness with others. May my actions today bear fruit that shows the beauty of Your goodness in the world around me.

UNSHAKEABLE FAITH

"Now faith is the assurance of things hoped for, the conviction of things not seen."
Hebrews 11:1

DEVOTIONAL

Faith is like a strong tree, standing tall even in the storm. Hebrews 11:1 teaches us that faith is believing in what we hope for, even if we can't see it yet. Just as we trust a friend to keep a promise, we can trust God to keep His promises too. Every prayer, every act of kindness, and every effort to love others helps our faith grow stronger. Let's remember to believe, even when things are tough!

DAILY REFLECTION

Think about a time when you felt a little scared or unsure about something, like a stormy day. How did you find comfort or strength? Can you think of a way to trust God and believe in His promises, just like you would trust a friend to keep their word?

PRAYER

Dear God, thank you for being like a strong tree that helps us stand tall, even when things feel stormy and unsure. Please help us to trust in Your promises, remember to love others, and grow our faith, just like we would trust a dear friend to keep their word.

CELEBRATING SMALL VICTORIES

"Do not despise these small beginnings, for the Lord rejoices to see the work begin." Zechariah 4:10 (NLT)

DEVOTIONAL

Every small victory counts! Just like planting a tiny seed that grows into a big tree, our little achievements matter to God. Zechariah 4:10 reminds us not to overlook the small beginnings in our lives. When you learn something new, share kindness, or take a step closer to your dreams, celebrate it! God loves to see our efforts. Each small step is part of a big journey with Him. Remember, every little act of faith brings us closer to His greatness.

DAILY REFLECTION

Reflect on a time when you achieved something small, like learning a new skill or helping someone. How did it make you feel, and why do you think those little victories are important on your journey with God?

PRAYER

Dear God, thank you for every small victory in our lives, like learning something new or showing kindness to others. Help us to remember that each little step we take brings us closer to You and reminds us of Your love and greatness.

SERVING WITH A JOYFUL HEART

"For we are God's handiwork, created in Christ Jesus to do good works, which God prepared in advance for us to do." Ephesians 2:10

DEVOTIONAL

Serving others is a special way to show God's love. In Ephesians 2:10, we learn that God created each of us with a purpose—to do good things! When we help others, we are not just being kind; we are shining God's light. Each small act of service brings joy, both to the person we are helping and to us. So, let's find joy in serving, knowing that we are fulfilling God's wonderful plan for our lives.

DAILY REFLECTION

How can you look for opportunities to serve others this week, and what small act of kindness can you do that might bring joy to someone else while also shining God's light?

PRAYER

Dear God, thank you for giving us hearts that can share your love through our actions. Help us to spot the small, special ways we can brighten someone's day and shine your light in the world around us.

WHEN GOD REDIRECTS YOUR PATH

"Trust in the Lord with all your heart and lean not on your own understanding; in all your ways acknowledge Him, and He will make your paths straight." — Proverbs 3:5-6

DEVOTIONAL

Have you ever felt lost and didn't know which way to go? God understands! Sometimes, He gently changes our plans to guide us toward something better. Proverbs 3:5-6 reminds us to trust God with all our hearts, even when things don't make sense. When we acknowledge Him in everything we do—our choices, our dreams, and our worries—He helps us find the right path. Remember, God's guidance can lead us to amazing adventures! Keep trusting Him!

DAILY REFLECTION

Think about a time when you felt uncertain about what to do next. How did you seek guidance during that time, and what did you learn about trusting God's plan for you?

PRAYER

Dear God, when we feel lost and unsure of which way to go, help us to trust in Your loving guidance and remember that You always have a better plan for us. Please light our path and give us the courage to follow You, knowing that with each step, we are on an amazing adventure together.

HEALED AND WHOLE IN CHRIST

"He heals the brokenhearted and binds up their wounds." Psalm 147:3

DEVOTIONAL

In life, we all face hurt and sadness, but we can trust that Jesus cares for us deeply. Psalm 147:3 reminds us, "He heals the brokenhearted and binds up their wounds." When we feel sad or alone, we can bring our feelings to Him in prayer. Jesus wants to comfort and heal us, making our hearts whole again. Remember, no matter how tough things seem, God is always with us, ready to help and love us completely.

DAILY REFLECTION

Reflect on a time when you felt sad or hurt. How did you bring those feelings to Jesus in prayer? What comfort or healing did you experience from Him during that time?

PRAYER

Dear Jesus, thank You for always being there to hold us close when our hearts feel heavy with sadness. Please help us to trust in Your loving care, as we share our feelings with You, knowing You are ready to comfort and heal us.

THE JOY OF OBEDIENCE

"Blessed are those who hear the word of God and obey it." Luke 11:28

"Blessed are those who hear the word of God and obey it." Luke 11:28

DEVOTIONAL

Obedience to God brings joy, just like when we help our parents or friends. In Luke 11:28, Jesus reminds us that when we hear God's word and do what it says, we are truly blessed. Think of it like following a treasure map—each step we take in obedience leads us closer to God's wonderful gifts. Let's listen to God today, doing our best to obey. In doing so, we will find happiness and grow in our faith!

DAILY REFLECTION

How does obeying God make you feel, and can you think of a time when following His word brought you joy, just like when you helped someone?

PRAYER

Dear God, thank you for your word that guides us like a treasure map, leading us to joy when we help others and obey you. Help us to listen and follow your teachings, so we can discover the wonderful gifts you have for us and feel the happiness that comes from being kind and loving.

COURAGE TO TRUST AGAIN

"Trust in the Lord with all your heart and lean not on your own understanding."
Proverbs 3:5

DEVOTIONAL

Sometimes, trusting others can be hard when we feel let down. God understands our feelings! Proverbs 3:5 reminds us to trust in Him completely, even when we don't see the whole picture. Just like a little bird learning to fly, it takes courage to take that leap of faith. Remember, God loves you and has wonderful plans for you. Let's pray together for the strength to trust Him again, knowing He is always here to guide us.

DAILY REFLECTION

How can you share your feelings of trust and doubt with God today, and what small step can you take to show that you are willing to trust Him a little bit more, like the bird learning to fly?

PRAYER

Dear God, help us to feel safe sharing our feelings of trust and doubt with You, knowing that You understand us fully. Please give us the courage to take small steps, like the little bird learning to fly, so we can trust Your loving plans for our lives.

RESTORING WHAT WAS LOST

"I will restore the years that the swarming locust has eaten." Joel 2:25

DEVOTIONAL

When we feel like we've lost joy or hope, remember God's promise in Joel 2:25: "I will restore the years that the swarming locust has eaten." Just as a gardener restores a barren field, God can bring new life to our hearts. Trust that He can heal our losses and fill our lives with blessings again. Take a moment today to pray and ask God to help you see His restoration in your life. You are never alone.

DAILY REFLECTION

Reflect on a time when you felt you had lost joy or hope. What are some ways you can see God working to restore your heart and fill your life with new blessings? Take a moment to write down your thoughts or share them with someone you trust. How can you invite God into that space for healing and restoration?

PRAYER

Dear God, when our hearts feel heavy and the joy seems distant, please help us remember Your promise to restore and bring new life, just like a gardener revives a barren field. May we feel Your loving presence as we trust in Your healing, and open our hearts to see the blessings You are preparing for us.

FINISHING THE MONTH FAITHFULLY

"Let us not become weary in doing good, for at the proper time we will reap a harvest if we do not give up." Galatians 6:9

DEVOTIONAL

As we finish this month, let's remember what Galatians 6:9 tells us: doing good is important, and we shouldn't get tired of it. Sometimes, we might feel like giving up, but God promises that if we keep going, we will see the results of our efforts. Each small act of kindness brings us closer to Him. Let's encourage each other to stay strong and keep doing good, knowing God has great things in store for us.

DAILY REFLECTION

As you think about what it means to do good and not give up, reflect on a time when you felt tired or discouraged. What helped you to keep going, and how can you encourage someone else who might feel the same way?

PRAYER

Dear God, thank You for reminding us that doing good is important, even when we feel tired or discouraged. Please help us to encourage each other and find strength in Your promises, knowing that our small acts of kindness can bring us closer to You and make a big difference in the world.

FAITH THAT PERSEVERES

"Let us not become weary in doing good, for at the proper time we will reap a harvest if we do not give up." Galatians 6:9

DEVOTIONAL

In our journey of faith, sometimes we feel tired or unsure, especially when doing good for others. Galatians 6:9 reminds us not to give up. Imagine planting seeds in a garden; they take time to grow. Just like that, our good deeds have their season. When we keep helping, loving, and being kind, God promises a wonderful harvest. Stay strong! Trust that your efforts matter. God is with you, so let's keep doing good together!

DAILY REFLECTION

As you think about the good things you do for others, how can you remind yourself that even small acts of kindness can lead to a big difference over time? What is one way you can keep going and trust in God's process, even when you feel tired or unsure?

PRAYER

Dear God, thank you for the small, kind things we can do for others, reminding us that every act of love can grow into something beautiful over time. Help us to stay strong and trust in Your promise as we continue to share our hearts and smiles with those around us.

GOD'S TIMING IS ALWAYS RIGHT

"He has made everything beautiful in its time." Ecclesiastes 3:11

DEVOTIONAL

God's timing is like a perfectly set clock. In Ecclesiastes 3:11, we learn that "He has made everything beautiful in its time." This means that God knows when things should happen in our lives. Sometimes, we might feel impatient or wish for things to change quickly. But remember, just as flowers bloom in their season, God is preparing wonderful things for you. Trust Him and be open to His plan. You'll see that waiting can lead to beautiful moments!

DAILY REFLECTION

How have you seen God working in your life through the waiting periods, and what beautiful moments have come from trusting in His timing?

PRAYER

Dear God, thank You for Your perfect timing, reminding us that just like a beautiful flower blooms when it's ready, You guide our lives with love and care. Help us to trust in Your plan and see the wonderful moments that come from waiting, knowing that each step is a part of Your beautiful design for us.

LIVING WITH OPEN HANDS

"Each of you should give what you have decided in your heart to give, not reluctantly or under compulsion, for God loves a cheerful giver." 2 Corinthians 9:7

DEVOTIONAL

Living with open hands means sharing what we have, whether it's time, talents, or treasures. God invites us to give joyfully, not out of pressure or duty. Imagine your heart as a basket; when you fill it with love and kindness, it overflows to others. Each act of giving, no matter how small, lights up the world around us. Let's choose to share cheerfully, reflecting God's love, and watch how He blesses both us and those we help.

DAILY REFLECTION

How can you fill your heart with love and kindness today, and in what small way can you share that with someone around you? Think about a time when you gave joyfully—what did that feel like, and how did it impact the person you shared with?

PRAYER

Dear God, help us to live with open hearts that overflow with love and kindness, so we can share our time, talents, and treasures with joy. May we always find small ways to brighten someone's day, reflecting Your love and bringing light to those around us. Amen.

THE POWER OF GOD'S WORD

"For the word of God is alive and active. It is sharper than any double-edged sword." Hebrews 4:12

DEVOTIONAL

God's Word is a powerful tool! In Hebrews 4:12, we learn that it is alive and can change our hearts. Just like a sword, God's Word helps us cut through our worries and fears, bringing clarity and hope. When we read the Bible, we get to hear God's voice and understand His love for us. Each time you open the Scriptures, remember that God is speaking directly to you, guiding you to grow closer to Him every day.

DAILY REFLECTION

How can you use God's Word to help you through a worry or fear you are facing right now? Consider a verse that brings you comfort, and think about how it might guide you closer to God.

PRAYER

Dear God, thank You for the gift of Your Word, which helps us understand Your love and guides us through our worries and fears. Please help us to remember that when we read the Bible, we hear Your voice and find the strength and comfort we need to grow closer to You every day.

ANCHORED IN HOPE

"We have this hope as an anchor for the soul, firm and secure."
Hebrews 6:19

DEVOTIONAL

When life feels like a wild storm, remember Hebrews 6:19: "We have this hope as an anchor for the soul, firm and secure." Just like a boat needs an anchor to stay steady, we need hope from God. This hope is Jesus, who promises to be with us always. When you feel lost or scared, hold on to that hope! Pray and trust in Him, and you will find peace in your heart, no matter what comes your way.

DAILY REFLECTION

Think about a time when you felt overwhelmed or scared, like you were in the middle of a storm. How can remembering that Jesus is your hope and anchor help you feel more secure in those moments? Write down your thoughts or share them with someone you trust.

PRAYER

Dear God, thank You for being our anchor of hope in life's storms. When we feel scared or lost, help us to remember that Jesus is always with us, filling our hearts with peace and strength.

TRUSTING GOD'S PROCESS

"Trust in the Lord with all your heart and lean not on your own understanding." Proverbs 3:5

DEVOTIONAL

Life can be confusing, and sometimes we don't understand why things happen the way they do. Proverbs 3:5 teaches us to trust the Lord with all our hearts. This means relying on Him, even when we don't see the whole picture. Imagine a puzzle—each piece has its place, but you can't see the beautiful image until it's complete. God's plan for you is like that puzzle. Trust Him to guide you, knowing He sees the full picture!

DAILY REFLECTION

What is one area in your life where you find it difficult to trust God, and how can remembering that He sees the complete picture help you approach that situation differently?

PRAYER

Dear God, sometimes life feels like a puzzle with pieces that don't seem to fit, and we ask for Your help in trusting Your plan for us. Please remind us that You see the complete picture, guiding us through our confusion and filling our hearts with peace.

PURPOSE IN THE PAIN

"And we know that in all things God works for the good of those who love him, who have been called according to his purpose." Romans 8:28

DEVOTIONAL

Sometimes, life can be tough, and we might feel sad or confused. But Romans 8:28 reminds us that God has a special purpose in our pain. He cares for us and works through our challenges to make us stronger and help us grow. When we trust Him, even our hardest moments can turn into something good. Remember, each struggle is a step on the journey God has for you, leading you closer to His love and purpose.

DAILY REFLECTION

Reflect on a time when you faced a difficult challenge. How did it make you feel, and what did you learn from that experience? In what ways can you see God working in your life through your struggles?

PRAYER

Dear God, thank you for being with us when life feels tough and confusing. Help us to trust in your love and see the good that can come from our struggles, knowing that you are always guiding us toward your special purpose.

FINDING REST IN SURRENDER

"Come to me, all you who are weary and burdened, and I will give you rest." Matthew 11:28

DEVOTIONAL

When we feel tired or worried, Jesus invites us to come to Him. In Matthew 11:28, He says, "Come to me, all you who are weary and burdened, and I will give you rest." This means we can share our worries with Him and let go of the weight we carry. Surrendering our worries to Jesus opens the door to peace and comfort. Today, take a moment to relax in His presence, knowing He cares for you deeply.

DAILY REFLECTION

Reflect on a time when you felt tired or worried. What specific worries or burdens would you like to share with Jesus today? How do you think surrendering those worries to Him can help you find peace and comfort? Take a moment to write down your thoughts or pray about it.

PRAYER

Dear Jesus, thank you for inviting us to come to You when we feel tired or worried. Please help us to share our burdens with You, knowing that Your love brings us the peace and comfort we long for.

SPIRITUAL REFRESHMENT

"Come to me, all you who are weary and burdened, and I will give you rest."
Matthew 11:28

DEVOTIONAL

When we feel tired or heavy with worries, Jesus invites us to come to Him. Just like a cozy blanket warms us, resting in Jesus refreshes our hearts. He understands our burdens and wants to lighten our loads. Take a moment today to talk to Him about what's on your mind. In prayer, you'll find comfort, peace, and new strength. Remember, Jesus is always ready to help you feel light and joyful again.

DAILY REFLECTION

What worries or burdens do you want to share with Jesus today, and how do you hope it will feel to rest in His care?

PRAYER

Dear Jesus, thank you for being there when I feel weary and worried, and help me to share my burdens with you so that I can find peace and strength. Please remind me that resting in your love is like a warm blanket, bringing comfort and joy to my heart.

A NEW SONG IN YOUR HEART

"Sing to the Lord a new song; sing to the Lord, all the earth." Psalm 96:1

DEVOTIONAL

God loves when we sing! Psalm 96:1 reminds us to sing a new song to the Lord. This doesn't always mean music; it can be a joyful heart. Each day, God gives us new blessings, like sunshine, laughter, and friends. When we notice these gifts, we can sing praises to Him in our hearts. Try thinking of ways God has blessed you today and share that joy with others. Let your new song shine brightly!

DAILY REFLECTION

What are three things that made you smile today, and how can you share that happiness with someone else?

PRAYER

Dear God, thank you for the beautiful blessings you give us each day — like sunshine, laughter, and the love of friends. Help us to sing our new song with joy in our hearts and to share the happiness we find with those around us.

CONFIDENT IN HIS CALLING

"Being confident of this, that he who began a good work in you will carry it on to completion until the day of Christ Jesus." Philippians 1:6

DEVOTIONAL

God loves you and has a special plan for your life. Philippians 1:6 reminds us that He started a good work in you, and He will help you grow every day. Sometimes, you might feel unsure or scared about the future, but remember, God is with you! Trust Him to complete the work He has begun. Stay close to Him through prayer and reading His Word, and watch how your faith flourishes as you lean on His promises.

DAILY REFLECTION

Reflect on a time when you felt unsure or scared about the future. How did you see God's love and guidance in that situation? What steps can you take to stay close to Him and trust His plan for your life?

PRAYER

Dear God, thank You for loving me and having a special plan for my life. When I feel scared or unsure about what's ahead, help me to trust in Your goodness and stay close to You through prayer and Your Word.

HEALING TAKES TIME

"But they that wait upon the Lord shall renew their strength; they shall mount up with wings as eagles; they shall run, and not be weary; and they shall walk, and not faint." Isaiah 40:31

DEVOTIONAL

Healing takes time, just like a seed growing into a tree. In Isaiah 40:31, God reminds us that when we wait on Him, He gives us strength. It's okay to feel tired or sad; those feelings are part of life. Just remember to pray, trust in God, and wait patiently. As we do this, God will lift us up, help us feel better, and guide us on our journey. Keep believing! God is always with you.

DAILY REFLECTION

As you think about how healing takes time, just like a seed growing into a tree, what is something you are waiting on God for in your life? How can you show trust and patience during this time?

PRAYER

Dear God, thank you for reminding us that healing takes time, just like a tiny seed grows into a strong tree. Help us to trust you and be patient as we wait for the good things you have planned for us, knowing that you are always by our side.

PEACE WHEN YOU DON'T UNDERSTAND

"Peace I leave with you; my peace I give you." John 14:27

DEVOTIONAL

Sometimes, life feels confusing, and we don't understand why things happen. In these moments, God reminds us that we can find peace in Him. Jesus says in John 14:27, "Peace I leave with you; my peace I give you." This means that when we trust God, even when we don't have all the answers, He fills our hearts with calmness and comfort. Just pause, pray, and let His peace wash over you, guiding you through any storm.

DAILY REFLECTION

Think about a time when you felt confused or uncertain about something in your life. How can you invite God's peace into that situation, trusting that He is with you even when the answers are not clear? Take a moment to reflect and write down what you feel or how you might approach it differently with God's guidance.

PRAYER

Dear God, thank you for being with us when life feels confusing and uncertain. Please help me to trust in your peace, even when I don't have all the answers, and fill my heart with your calmness as I navigate through difficult moments.

YOUR PRAYERS MATTER

"The prayer of a righteous person is powerful and effective." James 5:16

DEVOTIONAL

God loves to hear our prayers! James 5:16 tells us that when we pray, our prayers can be powerful and effective. This means that our words can bring comfort, healing, and change. Whether you pray for yourself, your family, or friends, know that every prayer matters. Take time today to talk to God about what's on your heart. Remember, He is always listening and eager to help you grow closer to Him through your prayers.

DAILY REFLECTION

What is something you would like to talk to God about today, and how do you think your prayer can help you or someone else?

PRAYER

Dear God, thank You for always listening to our prayers and for the love You show us every day. Help us to remember that our words can bring comfort and change, and guide us as we talk to You about what's in our hearts.

WHEN GOD FEELS DISTANT

"Draw near to God, and he will draw near to you." James 4:8

DEVOTIONAL

Sometimes, it feels like God is far away. But remember, He wants to be close to you! James 4:8 tells us, "Draw near to God, and he will draw near to you." This means when you pray, read the Bible, or take a quiet moment to think about Him, you are taking steps toward God. Even when it seems tough, keep reaching out. Your effort will open the door for Him to come closer and guide your heart.

DAILY REFLECTION

When you find yourself feeling distant from God, what are some simple ways you can take a step closer to Him today?

PRAYER

Dear God, sometimes I feel like You're far away, but I know You want to be close to me. Help me to take steps toward You today, whether through prayer, reading my Bible, or just thinking about You, so I can feel Your love and guidance in my heart.

HIS MERCY IS ENOUGH

"But he said to me, 'My grace is sufficient for you, for my power is made perfect in weakness.' Therefore I will boast all the more gladly about my weaknesses, so that Christ's power may rest on me." 2 Corinthians 12:9

DEVOTIONAL

In moments when we feel weak or unsure, remember that God's mercy is enough for us. He tells us that His grace is all we need, especially when we're struggling. When we face challenges, we can lean on Him and trust that He makes us strong. Our weaknesses show His power. Let's celebrate these moments, knowing that it's not about being perfect, but about relying on God's love and strength to guide us each day.

DAILY REFLECTION

In times when you feel weak or unsure, how can you consciously remind yourself to lean on God's grace and love? Reflect on a recent challenge you faced and think about how you can celebrate the strength that comes from relying on Him in those moments.

PRAYER

Dear God, help us to remember that in our times of weakness and uncertainty, Your love and grace are always there to lift us up. May we celebrate our challenges as opportunities to feel Your strength, trusting that You are with us every step of the way.

WALKING BOLDLY WITH GOD

"Be strong and courageous; do not be afraid, for the Lord your God will be with you wherever you go." Joshua 1:9

DEVOTIONAL

Walking boldly with God means trusting Him, even when things feel scary. In Joshua 1:9, God reminds us to be strong and brave because He is always with us. When we face challenges, like starting a new school or making new friends, we can remember that God is right beside us, giving us courage. Let's take each step with confidence, knowing that God loves us and helps us through everything we face. Trust Him today!

DAILY REFLECTION

Think about a time when you felt scared or unsure about something, like starting a new school or meeting new friends. How can you remember that God is with you in those moments, and what steps can you take to feel brave and trust Him?

PRAYER

Dear God, help us to be strong and brave when we face new and scary things, knowing that you are always by our side. Thank you for your love and support, guiding us to take confident steps as we trust in you each day.

LESS OF ME, MORE OF HIM

"He must increase, but I must decrease." John 3:30

DEVOTIONAL

In our lives, it's easy to focus on ourselves—what we want, how we feel. But John 3:30 reminds us that to grow closer to God, we must let Him take the lead. Think of it like a sunflower that turns to the sun for strength. When we shift our attention from ourselves to Jesus, we shine brighter with His love. Today, try sharing kindness, listening well, and praying more. The less we focus on ourselves, the more we can reflect Him!

DAILY REFLECTION

How can you turn your attention away from what you want today and focus on showing kindness to others instead? What is one small act of love you can do to reflect Jesus in your interactions?

PRAYER

Dear God, help me to turn my eyes away from my own wants and to see the needs of those around me. May every kind act and loving word I share reflect your light and love, drawing me closer to You.

THE JOY OF TRUSTING

"Trust in the Lord with all your heart and lean not on your own understanding."
Proverbs 3:5

DEVOTIONAL

Trusting in God is like a child holding a parent's hand while walking. Proverbs 3:5 reminds us to trust the Lord completely, believing He knows the best path for us. When we face challenges or don't understand things, it's okay to lean on God instead of our own thoughts. He loves us and wants to guide us. Today, take a moment to share your worries with Him and feel the joy of trusting in His perfect plan for you.

DAILY REFLECTION

How can you practice trusting in God like a child holding a parent's hand when you face a challenge or feel unsure? Think of a recent worry you had and write down how you can lean on God for support.

PRAYER

Dear God, thank you for holding my hand like a loving parent as I walk through life. Help me feel your presence when I'm unsure and remind me to trust in your perfect plan, knowing you always want what is best for me.

A LIGHT FOR THE WORLD

"Let your light shine before others, that they may see your good deeds and glorify your Father in heaven." Matthew 5:16

DEVOTIONAL

Every day, you have the chance to shine your light for others, just like stars in the night sky! Jesus tells us in Matthew 5:16 to let our good deeds show, so people can see the love of God through us. When you help someone, share kindness, or smile at a friend, you're shining your light brightly. Remember, your actions can inspire others to see God's love, making the world a brighter place. Let your light shine!

DAILY REFLECTION

Think about a time when you did something kind for someone or helped a friend. How did that make you feel inside, and how do you think it made them feel? How can you shine your light for others today?

PRAYER

Dear Jesus, thank you for the chance to shine our lights and show your love to others through our kind actions. Help us to remember the joy we feel when we help a friend and inspire us to share that light with everyone around us today.

SPIRIT-LED LIVING

"But if you are led by the Spirit, you are not under the law." Galatians 5:18

DEVOTIONAL

Living by the Spirit means letting God guide our thoughts and actions. In Galatians 5:18, we learn that when we follow the Spirit, we are free from the heavy weight of trying to be perfect. Instead, we focus on love, kindness, and joy. Each day, ask the Spirit to lead you —whether in choosing how to treat others or in making choices that honor God. Trust in His direction, and you'll find true freedom and peace in your journey with Him.

DAILY REFLECTION

As you reflect on the idea of living by the Spirit, consider this question: How can you invite the Spirit into your daily choices to ensure that your thoughts and actions reflect love, kindness, and joy? Take a moment to think about specific situations where you need guidance and how trusting in the Spirit might bring you peace and freedom in those moments.

PRAYER

Dear God, help me to open my heart and mind to Your Spirit, guiding my thoughts and actions so that I may share love, kindness, and joy with everyone I meet. In each choice I make today, remind me to trust in Your direction, finding peace and freedom in Your loving presence.

HE SEES EVERY TEAR

"He will wipe every tear from their eyes." Revelation 21:4

DEVOTIONAL

Life can be tough, and sometimes we feel sad or hurt. But remember, God loves you and sees every tear you cry. In Revelation 21:4, it says that He will wipe every tear from our eyes. This means that God cares about your feelings and wants to take away your pain. When you pray and share your heart with Him, you grow closer to Him. Trust that He is always there, ready to comfort you and bring joy back into your life.

DAILY REFLECTION

Think about a time when you felt sad or hurt. How did you feel knowing that God sees your tears and wants to comfort you? In what ways can you share your feelings with God through prayer?

PRAYER

Dear God, thank you for loving me and for always being there to see my tears and comfort my heart. Help me to share my feelings with you in prayer, knowing that You will bring joy and healing into my life.

THE BEAUTY OF DEPENDENCE

"Cast all your anxiety on him because he cares for you." 1 Peter 5:7

DEVOTIONAL

In life, it's easy to feel overwhelmed and alone. But remember, God invites us to share our worries with Him. When we "cast all our anxiety on him," we find comfort in His loving care. Picture a little bird being cradled by a strong hand—God's hands are there for us, too! Dependence on Him isn't weakness; it's a beautiful way to grow. Trust that God is big enough for your worries and loves you deeply. Lean on Him today!

DAILY REFLECTION

How can you take a moment today to share your worries with God, and what does it feel like to imagine Him holding you close like that bird in His hands?

PRAYER

Dear God, in moments when I feel overwhelmed, help me to remember that I can always share my worries with You, just like a little bird in Your gentle hands. Thank You for your loving care; let me feel Your presence and trust that You are always there to lift me up.

A LIFE OF OVERFLOW

"Whoever believes in me, as Scripture has said, rivers of living water will flow from within them." John 7:38

DEVOTIONAL

Imagine living with a heart full of joy and kindness, just like a river overflowing with fresh water! In John 7:38, Jesus promises that if we believe in Him, His love and spirit will fill us up and spill over into the lives of others. Each day, we can invite Jesus into our hearts, allowing His joy to flow out to friends and family. As we grow closer to Him, our lives can become a beautiful blessing for those around us.

DAILY REFLECTION

Think about a time when you felt happiness or kindness overflowing in your heart. How can you invite Jesus into your heart today so that His joy can spill over into your interactions with others? What is one small act of kindness you can do for someone around you?

PRAYER

Dear Jesus, thank You for filling our hearts with joy and kindness like a river that flows freely. Help us to invite Your spirit into our lives today, guiding us to share Your love through small acts of kindness with those around us.

THE LORD WILL PROVIDE

"And my God will supply every need of yours according to his riches in glory in Christ Jesus." Philippians 4:19

DEVOTIONAL

God loves you and knows what you need. In Philippians 4:19, we learn that He promises to provide for every need we have. Sometimes, we might worry about what's coming next, but we can trust that God sees us and cares for us. Whether it's a friend to play with or help in school, God is always there. Let's thank Him for His goodness and trust that He will give us what we need today and always.

DAILY REFLECTION

Think about a time when you were worried about something you needed, like a friend to talk to or help with a tough subject in school. How did you feel in that moment, and how can remembering that God knows your needs help you feel more at peace now?

PRAYER

Dear God, thank you for loving me and knowing everything I need, even when I feel worried or unsure. Please help me to trust that you are always there to provide for my needs and to fill my heart with peace.

STANDING IN SPIRITUAL AUTHORITY

"Be strong in the Lord and in His mighty power." Ephesians 6:10

DEVOTIONAL

Standing in spiritual authority means trusting God's strength in your life. Ephesians 6:10 reminds us to be strong in the Lord and His mighty power. Imagine standing tall like a superhero, knowing you have God's help. When challenges arise or fears creep in, remember to pray and ask for His strength. By relying on God, you can face anything! Each day, let His power guide your actions and choices, helping you grow closer to Him and shine His light.

DAILY REFLECTION

How does knowing you can rely on God's strength change the way you face your daily challenges? Think of a recent situation where you felt afraid or uncertain. How could you invite God into that moment to help you stand tall and confident?

PRAYER

Dear God, thank you for being our mighty strength and helping us stand tall like superheroes. When we feel afraid or unsure, remind us to invite you into those moments so we can face our challenges with your love and courage.

FAITH OVER FRUSTRATION

"Trust in the Lord with all your heart and lean not on your own understanding."
Proverbs 3:5

DEVOTIONAL

When things don't go your way, it's easy to feel frustrated. But Proverbs 3:5 reminds us to "Trust in the Lord with all your heart." This means we can choose to have faith instead of letting difficulties upset us. When challenges arise, take a moment to pray and ask God for help. Trust that He knows what's best for you. By leaning on His understanding, you'll find peace and strength to face any situation with confidence.

DAILY REFLECTION

When you face a challenge or something doesn't go as you hoped, how can you remind yourself to trust in God and find peace in that moment? What is one way you can ask Him for help?

PRAYER

Dear God, when things don't go as I hope and I feel upset, help me to remember to trust in You with all my heart. Please give me Your peace and strength to face my challenges, and remind me to ask for Your guidance whenever I need it.

RENEWED BY GRACE

"Therefore, if anyone is in Christ, he is a new creation; the old has passed away, behold, the new has come." 2 Corinthians 5:17

DEVOTIONAL

God loves us so much that He wants to give us a fresh start. When we choose to follow Jesus, we become new creations! This means our old mistakes and hurts are forgiven, and we can begin again. Imagine planting a seed; as it grows, it becomes a beautiful flower. Just like that, when we let God into our hearts, He helps us grow and change for the better. Embrace this new life and let His grace renew you every day.

DAILY REFLECTION

How can you embrace the fresh start that God offers you and let His love help you grow and change for the better in your life?

PRAYER

Dear God, thank you for loving us so much and giving us the chance to start fresh with you. Help us to embrace the beautiful changes you bring to our hearts, so we can grow and shine like a lovely flower in your garden.

THE GIFT OF HIS PRESENCE

"For where two or three gather in my name, there am I with them." Matthew 18:20

DEVOTIONAL

When we gather with friends or family to talk about God, something special happens. Jesus promised that when we come together in His name, He is right there with us. This means we don't have to feel alone; His presence fills our hearts and makes our time together joyful. Whenever you meet with others to pray, share stories, or read the Bible, remember—you are never alone. Embrace His gift of presence and let it guide your journey with Him.

DAILY REFLECTION

Reflect on a time when you gathered with friends or family to talk about God. How did you feel during that time? In what ways did you sense Jesus' presence among you? Consider how these moments shape your relationship with Him and with others. What can you do to create more of these special gatherings in your life?

PRAYER

Dear Jesus, thank You for being with us when we gather with our friends and family to share our love for You. Help us to always remember Your presence in our hearts and to create more moments together where we can celebrate Your joy and love.

FINISH STRONG IN FAITH

"I have fought the good fight, I have finished the race, I have kept the faith."
2 Timothy 4:7

DEVOTIONAL

In life, we all have challenges, just like a race. Paul reminds us to "fight the good fight" and "finish strong" in our faith. Each day is a chance to trust God more and live out His love. When we face difficulties, we can remember that God is by our side, helping us keep going. Let's encourage one another to stay strong in our faith, knowing that God rewards those who finish the race with Him.

DAILY REFLECTION

Reflect on a recent challenge you faced in your life. How did you feel in that moment, and how did you see God's presence helping you through? What steps can you take to encourage someone else who might be facing a similar challenge in their faith journey?

PRAYER

Dear God, thank You for being with us as we face life's challenges, just like runners in a race. Help us to trust in Your love and strength, so we can encourage one another to keep going and finish strong in our faith.

Halfway Through Our Journey

You are now halfway through this devotional journey.

Many women discover this book through the thoughtful reviews shared by readers like you.

If these pages have supported your faith and daily reflection, would you consider sharing a short review on Amazon?

Your voice may help someone else find encouragement today.

devo.anchoredgraces.com/workingmoms

FREEDOM IN CHRIST

"So if the Son sets you free, you will be free indeed." John 8:36

DEVOTIONAL

Freedom in Christ is a beautiful gift! In John 8:36, we learn that when Jesus sets us free, we are truly free. This means we don't have to carry our worries or mistakes. Instead, we can trust Him with everything, knowing He loves us. Every day, remember that you can let go of anything that holds you back. Jesus is always with you, helping you grow and guiding you on the path of His love. Celebrate your freedom!

DAILY REFLECTION

As you think about the freedom you have in Christ, what is one thing you can let go of today that is holding you back from experiencing His love and guidance fully?

PRAYER

Dear Jesus, thank you for the wonderful gift of freedom that you give us, reminding us that we can let go of our worries and mistakes. Help me to trust you more each day and to release anything that holds me back from fully experiencing your love and guidance.

GOD'S LOVE NEVER FAILS

"Give thanks to the Lord, for he is good; his love endures forever." Psalm 136:1

DEVOTIONAL

God's love is like a warm blanket that wraps us up and makes us feel safe. In Psalm 136:1, we learn that God is good and His love never goes away. Just like the sun shines every day, God's love is always there for us, even when things are tough. Let's remember to give thanks for His never-ending love. Today, take a moment to say, "Thank you, God, for loving me always!" Your heart will feel happy!

DAILY REFLECTION

How can you remind yourself of God's everlasting love when you face tough times, and what is one thing you can do today to show gratitude for that love?

PRAYER

Dear God, thank you for your love that wraps around us like a warm blanket, keeping us safe and secure. Help me to remember your kindness in tough times and show my gratitude today by sharing a smile with someone, just as your love brings joy to my heart.

COURAGE TO FOLLOW GOD'S CALL

"Have I not commanded you? Be strong and courageous. Do not be afraid; do not be discouraged, for the LORD your God will be with you wherever you go." Joshua 1:9

DEVOTIONAL

When God calls you to do something special, it can feel scary. But remember, He tells us to be strong and brave! Just like He promised Joshua, God promises to be with you no matter where you go. Think about how you can show courage today—maybe by standing up for a friend or trying something new. Trust that God is by your side, helping you take those brave steps to follow His path. You are never alone!

DAILY REFLECTION

Think about a time when you felt scared to do something new or stand up for someone. What is one brave step you can take today to show courage, knowing that God is with you every step of the way?

PRAYER

Dear God, thank you for always being with us, even when things feel scary. Please help us to be brave like Joshua, showing courage as we stand up for our friends and try new things, knowing you are guiding us every step of the way.

TRUE FREEDOM THROUGH FAITH

"Therefore if the Son makes you free, you shall be free indeed." John 8:36 (NKJV)

DEVOTIONAL

True freedom comes from knowing Jesus! In John 8:36, we learn that when the Son sets us free, we are really free. This means we don't have to be trapped by worry, fear, or mistakes. Trusting Jesus opens our hearts to His love and gives us joy. Think of a bird soaring in the sky—free and light! Today, remember that faith in Jesus frees us to live fully, with peace and hope. Embrace that freedom and share it with others!

DAILY REFLECTION

How can trusting Jesus help you feel lighter and more free in your everyday life? Think about a time when you felt weighed down by worry or fear—what would it look like to let go of that burden and embrace the freedom that comes from knowing Him?

PRAYER

Dear Jesus, thank you for setting us free and filling our hearts with your love and joy. Help us to trust in you each day, letting go of our worries and fears so we can soar like a bird, feeling light and full of hope.

FAITH IN THE EVERYDAY

"So we fix our eyes not on what is seen, but on what is unseen, since what is seen is temporary, but what is unseen is eternal." 2 Corinthians 4:18

DEVOTIONAL

Faith helps us see the bigger picture in our daily lives. When we face challenges or feel sad, it's easy to focus on what we can see around us. But God reminds us in 2 Corinthians 4:18 that we should look beyond our troubles. The things we see are temporary, but God's love and our hope in Him are forever. Let's trust in His promises and keep our hearts open to the wonderful things He has planned for us!

DAILY REFLECTION

Reflect on a recent challenge you faced. How did it make you feel in the moment, and what was your focus? Now, think about how your faith can help you see this situation from a bigger perspective. In what ways can trusting in God's promises change how you view your current struggles?

PRAYER

Dear God, thank you for being our guiding light when we feel overwhelmed by life's challenges. Help us to remember that while our troubles may seem big, your love and promises are forever, and you have wonderful plans for us that we can trust in.

ABIDING IN PEACE

"Peace I leave with you; my peace I give to you." John 14:27

DEVOTIONAL

Abiding in peace means resting in God's love and faithfulness. In John 14:27, Jesus promises us His peace—a deep, calming feeling that the world can't give. When we face worries, let's remember that His peace is like a gentle hug, comforting us in tough times. To experience this peace, we can pray, read the Bible, and trust Him with our fears. As we seek Him daily, His peace will fill our hearts and guide our steps.

DAILY REFLECTION

How can you invite God's peace into your daily life, especially when worries start to creep in? Consider ways you can pray, read the Bible, or simply trust Him with your fears this week.

PRAYER

Dear God, thank you for your promise of peace that comforts our hearts like a gentle hug. Help us to rest in your love and trust you with our worries, so we can feel your calming presence in our daily lives.

LIVING FOR AN AUDIENCE OF ONE

"Whatever you do, work heartily, as for the Lord and not for men." Colossians 3:23

DEVOTIONAL

In everything you do, remember to work for God, not just to please others. When you help, share, or learn, think of it as a gift to Him. This means doing your best, even when no one is watching. God sees your hard work, and it makes Him smile. As you strive to live for Him, you'll find joy and purpose in each task. Trust that your efforts matter and are part of His beautiful plan for you.

DAILY REFLECTION

When you think about the things you do each day, how can you make sure that you are doing them to honor God, rather than just to make someone else happy? What small actions can you take to see your efforts as gifts to Him?

PRAYER

Dear God, help me to remember that every good thing I do is a gift to You, not just to make others smile. Teach me to find joy and purpose in my actions, knowing that my hard work brings You happiness, even when no one is watching.

FINDING STILLNESS WITH GOD

"Be still, and know that I am God." Psalm 46:10

DEVOTIONAL

Finding stillness with God can be like a warm hug for your heart. Psalm 46:10 tells us, "Be still, and know that I am God." This means taking a moment to pause, breathe, and listen to God. When we find quiet spaces in our day, we can hear His gentle voice. Try closing your eyes and thanking Him for His love. In those moments of stillness, you'll feel His presence and grow closer to Him, finding peace in your heart.

DAILY REFLECTION

Take a moment to sit in a quiet place. As you close your eyes, think about a time you felt close to God. What did that moment look like for you? How did it make your heart feel? In what ways can you create more spaces for stillness in your daily life to strengthen that connection?

PRAYER

Dear God, thank you for the warm hug of your presence that brings peace to my heart. Help me to find quiet moments in my day so I can listen to your gentle voice and feel your love fill me up.

THE STRENGTH OF SURRENDER

"Come to me, all you who are weary and burdened, and I will give you rest."
Matthew 11:28

DEVOTIONAL

When we feel tired and worried, Jesus invites us to come to Him. Surrendering our burdens means letting go of what weighs us down and trusting God to take care of us. Just like a child who rests in a parent's arms, we can find comfort in God's love. When we share our struggles with Him, He gives us peace and strength. Today, take a moment to surrender your worries and let Jesus fill you with His rest.

DAILY REFLECTION

Think about a worry or burden that has been on your mind lately. How can you take a moment today to surrender that to Jesus and trust Him to carry it for you? What feelings come up as you imagine resting in His love and letting go of what weighs you down?

PRAYER

Dear Jesus, when I feel tired and worried, I come to You and lay down my burdens, trusting in Your love to lift me up. Help me to find peace in Your arms, knowing that I can rest in Your care and let go of what weighs me down.

BECOMING A WOMAN OF INFLUENCE

"She opens her mouth with wisdom, and the teaching of kindness is on her tongue."
Proverbs 31:26

DEVOTIONAL

In Proverbs 31:26, we learn about a woman of influence who speaks wisdom and kindness. Imagine how powerful your words can be! Every time you speak to someone, you have the chance to uplift and encourage them. Ask God to help you choose words that bring joy and comfort. Remember, sharing kindness not only helps others feel loved but also grows your own heart closer to God. Let's aim to be wise and kind in all we say!

DAILY REFLECTION

Reflect on a time when your words made someone feel good. How can you use your words today to encourage and uplift someone else?

PRAYER

Dear God, please help me to choose words that bring joy and comfort to those around me, just like the wise woman in Proverbs. May my words lift others up and strengthen my heart, drawing me closer to you as I spread kindness and encouragement each day.

TRUST WHEN YOU CAN'T SEE

"For we walk by faith, not by sight." 2 Corinthians 5:7

DEVOTIONAL

Sometimes, life feels like walking in a dark room. We can't see everything around us, and that can be scary. But God tells us to trust Him, even when we can't see the way ahead. Just like we believe the ground is there when we take a step, we can believe that God is with us. Remember, faith is trusting in His love and plans for us. Let go of fear, and take that step with courage!

DAILY REFLECTION

Think about a time when you felt unsure or scared, like you were in a dark room. How did you find the courage to keep moving forward? What does trusting God look like for you in those moments?

PRAYER

Dear God, sometimes we find ourselves in dark places where we feel afraid and unsure, but we trust that You are always with us, guiding our steps. Help us to let go of our fears and to walk forward with faith, knowing that Your love lights our way.

GRACE THAT COVERS ALL

"But where sin increased, grace abounded all the more." Romans 5:20

DEVOTIONAL

In Romans 5:20, we learn that no mistake is too big for God's grace. When we mess up or feel sad, God's love is bigger than our worries. Imagine grace like a warm blanket that covers every hurt and wrong choice. Each day is a chance to start fresh and feel God's loving presence. Remember, no matter what happens, His grace will always surround you. Trust in that love and let it help you grow closer to Him.

DAILY REFLECTION

How can you remind yourself of God's grace when you feel anxious or make a mistake, and what are some small ways you can focus on His love each day?

PRAYER

Dear God, thank you for your amazing grace that wraps around us like a warm blanket, reminding us that every mistake is met with your love. Help us to feel your presence in our hearts each day, guiding us to trust in your kindness and to embrace the new beginnings you offer us.

LETTING GOD LEAD

"Trust in the Lord with all your heart and lean not on your own understanding." Proverbs 3:5

DEVOTIONAL

In life, there are many paths we can take, and sometimes we don't know which way to go. Proverbs 3:5 reminds us to trust in the Lord with all our hearts. This means letting God guide us, even when we feel unsure. When we lean on Him instead of just our own thoughts, He shows us the right steps to take. Today, take a moment to pray and ask God to lead you. Trust Him—He knows the way!

DAILY REFLECTION

Think about a time when you felt unsure about a decision or path you were facing. How did you invite God into that situation, and what did you feel as you trusted Him to guide you? What steps can you take today to lean on Him more in your daily choices?

PRAYER

Dear God, thank You for always being there to guide us when we feel unsure about which path to take. Help us to trust in You with our whole hearts, knowing that You will show us the right steps to take in every moment of our lives.

REJOICING IN TRIALS

"Consider it pure joy, my brothers and sisters, whenever you face trials of many kinds." James 1:2

DEVOTIONAL

When troubles come, it can feel tough and sad. But James reminds us to find joy in these moments! Why? Because challenges help us grow and learn. Think of a butterfly breaking free from its cocoon; it must struggle to become beautiful. Your faith can grow strong during hard times, too. So, when you face a trial, remember to smile and trust God. He is building you up, helping you become the amazing person He created you to be.

DAILY REFLECTION

When you encounter a tough situation, how can you remember to find joy in the struggle, just like the butterfly emerging from its cocoon? What steps can you take to trust God and see these challenges as opportunities for growth?

PRAYER

Dear God, when I face tough moments, help me remember that, like the butterfly, my struggles are a part of growing into the amazing person you created me to be. Fill my heart with joy and strength, so I can trust you and see these challenges as chances to learn and flourish. Amen.

THE POWER OF SPIRITUAL DISCIPLINE

"Train yourself to be godly." 1 Timothy 4:7

DEVOTIONAL

In 1 Timothy 4:7, we're reminded to "train yourself to be godly." Just like an athlete practices to grow stronger, we also need to practice our faith. This means spending time in prayer, reading the Bible, and worshiping God. By doing these things regularly, we become closer to God and learn to live in love and kindness. Each small effort builds a deeper relationship with Him. Let's train our hearts to seek Him every day!

DAILY REFLECTION

How can you make a small change in your daily routine to practice your faith and grow closer to God? What is one thing you can do this week to "train your heart" in love and kindness?

PRAYER

Dear God, help us to train our hearts to seek You each day, just as athletes train their bodies to grow stronger. May our small efforts in prayer, reading Your Word, and showing kindness bring us closer to You and fill our lives with love.

YOUR PAST DOES NOT DEFINE YOU

"Therefore, if anyone is in Christ, the new creation has come: The old has gone, the new is here!" 2 Corinthians 5:17

DEVOTIONAL

Have you ever felt like your mistakes from the past are too heavy to carry? Remember, when you believe in Jesus, you become a new creation! 2 Corinthians 5:17 reminds us that God gives us a fresh start. Your past doesn't define who you are today. Instead, God sees you as new and full of potential. Embrace this truth, and let it inspire you to grow in your faith. Each day is a chance to become more like Christ.

DAILY REFLECTION

Reflect on a time when you felt weighed down by past mistakes. How does knowing that you are a new creation in Christ change the way you see those experiences? Think about one step you can take today to embrace your fresh start and grow in your faith.

PRAYER

Dear God, thank you for your love that makes us new and gives us the strength to let go of our past mistakes. Help us to embrace each day as a fresh start filled with your grace, guiding us to grow closer to you.

CHOOSING JOY OVER ANXIETY

"Rejoice in the Lord always; again I will say, rejoice." Philippians 4:4

DEVOTIONAL

When we feel worried or anxious, it can be hard to find joy. But God asks us to rejoice always, even in tough times. Philippians 4:4 reminds us that joy is a choice we can make. Whenever you feel anxious, take a moment to think about all the good things God has done for you. You can choose to focus on those blessings and share your joy with others. Remember, God is always with you, and His joy is your strength!

DAILY REFLECTION

Think about a time when you felt worried or anxious. What good things has God done for you in that situation? How can you share those blessings with someone else today?

PRAYER

Dear God, thank you for always being with us, even when we feel worried or anxious. Help us to remember the good things you have done and to share our joy with others, knowing that you are our strength.

DELIGHT IN THE LORD

"Delight yourself in the Lord, and he will give you the desires of your heart." Psalm 37:4

DEVOTIONAL

Delighting in the Lord means finding joy in spending time with Him. When you pray, read the Bible, or enjoy nature, you are connecting with God. He loves to see us happy and fulfilled. As we grow closer to Him, our hearts begin to align with His desires. Trust that God knows what you truly need and want. When you seek Him first, He promises to bless you with beautiful gifts—far beyond what you can imagine!

DAILY REFLECTION

How do you feel when you spend time in prayer or reading the Bible? Can you think of a moment when you felt especially close to God and joyful?

PRAYER

Dear God, thank you for the joy that comes from spending time with You. Help me to find delight in our moments together, whether in prayer, reading Your Word, or enjoying the beauty of nature around me.

FINDING BALANCE IN GOD'S DESIGN

"Trust in the Lord with all your heart and lean not on your own understanding."
Proverbs 3:5

DEVOTIONAL

Finding balance in our lives can be tough, but God helps us! Proverbs 3:5 reminds us to trust in the Lord with all our heart. When we lean on our own understanding, we might feel confused or lost. Instead, let's seek God's guidance in everything we do. When we pray and read the Bible, we can discover His plan for us. Trusting God helps us find peace and balance, making our hearts joyful and strong.

DAILY REFLECTION

Reflect on a time when you faced confusion or felt overwhelmed in your life. How did seeking God's guidance through prayer or reading the Bible help you find clarity or balance in that situation? What steps can you take to ensure you continue to rely on Him in your daily life?

PRAYER

Dear God, thank you for being our guide when life feels confusing or overwhelming. Help us to trust in You and seek Your wisdom every day, so we can find peace and balance in our hearts.

HOPE IN THE WILDERNESS

"Those who hope in the Lord will renew their strength." Isaiah 40:31

DEVOTIONAL

In life, we sometimes find ourselves in tough situations, like being in a wilderness. When things feel hard, remember Isaiah 40:31: "Those who hope in the Lord will renew their strength." This means that when we trust in God, He fills us with new energy and courage. Just like a tired runner gets a boost from cheering fans, God lifts our spirits. Let's take a moment each day to pray and trust Him, finding hope even in difficult times.

DAILY REFLECTION

Think about a time when you faced a tough situation that felt overwhelming. How did you find strength to keep going, and how can trusting in God help you in similar situations in the future?

PRAYER

Dear God, thank you for being our source of strength when times are tough and for reminding us that we can always trust in you. Help us to find hope in the wilderness of life, just like a runner feels renewed energy from kind cheers, knowing you are always cheering us on.

YOU ARE GOD'S MASTERPIECE

"For we are God's masterpiece, created in Christ Jesus to do good works, which God prepared in advance for us to do." Ephesians 2:10

DEVOTIONAL

You are a masterpiece, just like a beautiful painting created by God. In Ephesians 2:10, we learn that God made you special to do good things. Every day, He has a plan for you, filled with opportunities to shine your light and help others. Remember, you are unique and loved, and God has equipped you to share love and kindness in the world. Trust Him, step into your purpose, and let your masterpiece shine brightly!

DAILY REFLECTION

What is one way you can share your unique gifts with someone today to help them feel loved and appreciated?

PRAYER

Dear God, thank you for making me special and unique, just like a beautiful painting. Please help me to shine my light today by using my gifts to show love and kindness to others, sharing your masterpiece with the world.

LIVING LOVED AND KNOWN

"For I know the plans I have for you, declares the Lord, plans to prosper you and not to harm you, plans to give you hope and a future." Jeremiah 29:11

DEVOTIONAL

God has a special plan just for you! This verse from Jeremiah reminds us that He knows each of our hearts and dreams. When you feel unsure or scared, remember that God loves you and wants what's best for you. His plans are full of hope and joy! Trust that you are not alone; He walks with you every day, guiding you toward a bright future. Embrace His love, and let it fill your heart with peace.

DAILY REFLECTION

Reflect on a time when you felt uncertain or scared about something in your life. How did remembering that God has a special plan for you help you find peace and courage? What steps can you take this week to trust in His guidance as you face new challenges?

PRAYER

Dear God, thank you for loving me and for the special plan you have just for me. Help me to remember that even when I am scared or unsure, you are with me every step of the way, guiding me with your love and filling my heart with peace.

THE VOICE THAT CALMS

"Peace I leave with you; my peace I give you." John 14:27

DEVOTIONAL

In our busy lives, it's easy to feel overwhelmed. But Jesus offers us a special gift: His peace. In John 14:27, He promises, "Peace I leave with you; my peace I give you." Imagine a calming voice whispering to you when things get tough, reminding you that you are loved and never alone. Whenever you feel anxious or scared, take a moment to breathe, pray, and listen for His soothing words. Trust in His peace today.

DAILY REFLECTION

When you find yourself feeling overwhelmed or anxious, how can you take a moment to connect with Jesus and remember the peace He promises? What does that quiet moment look like for you?

PRAYER

Dear Jesus, thank you for your promise of peace when life feels busy and overwhelming. Help us to take a moment to breathe, listen, and remember that you are always with us, bringing calm to our hearts.

RETURNING TO YOUR FIRST LOVE

"Yet I hold this against you: You have forsaken the love you had at first." Revelation 2:4

DEVOTIONAL

In Revelation 2:4, God reminds us about our first love for Him. Imagine how joyful you felt when you first learned about His amazing love! Sometimes, we get busy and forget to spend time with Him. To return to your first love, try setting aside time each day for prayer or reading the Bible. Talk to God like you would a friend, and remember how special your relationship with Him is. He loves you deeply and wants to grow closer with you!

DAILY REFLECTION

Reflect on a time when you felt a strong connection with God. What activities or practices helped you grow closer to Him? How can you incorporate those into your daily routine to deepen your relationship and return to that initial joy?

PRAYER

Dear God, thank you for your amazing love that fills my heart with joy. Help me to set aside time each day to pray and read your Word, so I can feel that special connection with you and remember the happiness of being close to you.

PERSEVERANCE THROUGH PRAYER

"Pray without ceasing." 1 Thessalonians 5:17

DEVOTIONAL

In 1 Thessalonians 5:17, we learn to "pray without ceasing." This means talking to God anytime and about everything! Whether you're happy, sad, or worried, God loves to hear from you. Think of prayer like a friend you can call on at any moment. When we keep our hearts open to God through prayer, we grow closer to Him. Remember, persevering in prayer helps us feel His love and guidance, even in tough times. Keep praying, and watch your faith blossom!

DAILY REFLECTION

How can you make prayer a regular part of your day, and what are some moments when you can reach out to God, whether you are feeling joyful or facing a challenge?

PRAYER

Dear God, thank you for listening to us anytime we want to talk, whether we feel happy or need a little help. Please help us remember to pray throughout our day, so we can feel your love and grow closer to you in every moment.

FLOURISHING IN EVERY SEASON

"Those who are planted in the house of the Lord shall flourish in the courts of our God." Psalm 92:13

DEVOTIONAL

In every season of life, we can grow strong and beautiful like a tree when we are rooted in God. Psalm 92:13 reminds us that when we are close to God, we flourish no matter what is happening around us. Just like flowers bloom in spring and trees stand tall in winter, we can find joy and strength in all moments. Let's trust God, spend time with Him, and watch how we blossom wherever we are!

DAILY REFLECTION

Reflect on a time when you felt strong and joyful despite difficult circumstances. What role did your connection with God play in helping you flourish during that season? How can you deepen that connection to continue growing in your faith?

PRAYER

Dear God, thank you for being like the roots of a mighty tree that keep us strong and steady, no matter the season we find ourselves in. Help us to spend time with you, so we can grow joyful and beautiful, blooming like flowers even when times are tough.

GOD'S PRESENCE IN YOUR ROUTINE

"Do not be afraid, for I am with you; do not be discouraged, for I am your God." Isaiah 41:10

DEVOTIONAL

Every day can feel similar, but remember, God is with you in every moment! Whether you're getting ready for school, playing with friends, or doing chores at home, God is by your side. When you feel scared or worried, think of Isaiah 41:10: "Do not be afraid, for I am with you." Talk to God in your routine, asking for strength and courage. Invite Him into your day, and you'll feel His love and guidance in everything you do.

DAILY REFLECTION

How can you invite God into your daily activities today, and what are some moments when you might need His strength and courage?

PRAYER

Dear God, thank you for being with me in every moment of my day, whether I'm at school, playing, or helping at home. Please fill my heart with strength and courage whenever I feel scared or unsure, so I can feel your love and guidance in all that I do.

LIVING WITH HOLY CONFIDENCE

"For we live by faith, not by sight." 2 Corinthians 5:7

DEVOTIONAL

Living with holy confidence means trusting God even when we can't see what's ahead. In 2 Corinthians 5:7, we learn that our journey isn't based on what we see, but on faith. Like walking in a dark room, we may not always know the way, but God is our guide. Each step taken in trust brings us closer to Him. Let's practice looking beyond our fears and uncertainties, believing that God is leading us to something wonderful.

DAILY REFLECTION

As you think about your life and the times when you felt uncertain or afraid, how can you practice trusting God more fully in those moments when you can't see the way ahead? What steps can you take to embrace faith instead of fear?

PRAYER

Dear God, help us to trust in You even when the path ahead seems unclear, knowing that You are always with us and guiding our steps. Teach us to embrace faith over fear, believing that each uncertain moment brings us closer to Your wonderful plans for our lives.

RELEASING THE WEIGHTS YOU CARRY

"Come to me, all you who are weary and burdened, and I will give you rest."
Matthew 11:28

DEVOTIONAL

When you feel tired or worried, remember what Jesus tells us in Matthew 11:28: "Come to me, all you who are weary and burdened, and I will give you rest." Imagine carrying a heavy backpack filled with rocks. That's what our worries can feel like. But Jesus invites us to let go of those weights. Take a moment to pray, share your troubles with Him, and feel His peace filling you. Trust that He will bring you comfort and strength.

DAILY REFLECTION

When you feel weary or worried, what are some of the "rocks" in your backpack that you can share with Jesus in prayer? How do you think it would feel to let go of those worries and trust in His comfort?

PRAYER

Dear Jesus, when my heart feels heavy and my mind is filled with worries, I come to You and share my burdens. Please help me let go of my troubles and fill me with Your peace and strength, so I can feel lighter and loved.

FAITH THAT TRANSFORMS

"Therefore, if anyone is in Christ, he is a new creation; the old has passed away, behold, the new has come." - 2 Corinthians 5:17

DEVOTIONAL

When we believe in Jesus, something amazing happens! In 2 Corinthians 5:17, the Bible says we become new creations. This means that old worries and mistakes don't define us anymore. With faith, we can let go of the past and embrace the wonderful life God has for us. Each day, remember that God is always with you, helping you grow and change. Trust in Him, and watch how your heart and life transform in beautiful ways!

DAILY REFLECTION

How can you let go of something from your past that has been holding you back, and what new possibilities do you think God is inviting you to embrace today?

PRAYER

Dear God, thank you for making us new creations in Jesus and for helping us let go of our past worries and mistakes. Please guide our hearts to trust in Your love each day, embracing the beautiful possibilities You have in store for us.

PRAISE BEFORE THE BREAKTHROUGH

"Let everything that has breath praise the Lord! Praise the Lord!"
Psalm 150:6

DEVOTIONAL

When we face tough times, it can be hard to feel joyful. But God invites us to praise Him even before we see answers to our prayers. In Psalm 150:6, we are reminded that everything that breathes should praise the Lord. Praising God isn't just for happy moments; it builds our faith. Let's choose to thank Him, trusting that He hears us and cares. As we lift our voices in praise, we open our hearts to His amazing breakthroughs.

DAILY REFLECTION

Reflect on a challenging situation in your life where you've struggled to feel joy. How might praising God in that moment change your perspective and help you trust in His goodness, even if you don't see immediate answers to your prayers?

PRAYER

Dear God, even when times are tough and joy feels far away, help us remember to praise You and trust in Your goodness. May our hearts open to Your love as we lift our voices in gratitude, believing that You are always with us and will bring hope in every situation.

NEW BEGINNINGS WITH GOD

"Your word is a lamp to my feet and a light to my path." Psalm 119:105

DEVOTIONAL

God's Word is like a special flashlight that helps us see the right path in life. Just as we need light to avoid stumbling in the dark, we need the Bible to guide us. When we read and understand God's truths, we learn how to make good choices and follow Him. Take time each day to enjoy His word, and let it lead you—trust that God will always be with you, lighting your way.

DAILY REFLECTION

How can you use what you read in the Bible to help you make a tough choice you might face this week?

PRAYER

Dear God, thank you for giving us Your Word to guide us like a special flashlight, helping us see the right path in our lives. Please help us to read and understand your truths every day, so we can make good choices and trust that You are always lighting our way.

CONFIDENCE IN HIS PLAN

"For I know the plans I have for you, declares the Lord, plans to prosper you and not to harm you, plans to give you hope and a future." Jeremiah 29:11

DEVOTIONAL

God has a special plan for each of us, just like He promised in Jeremiah 29:11. Sometimes we may feel lost or unsure, but we can trust that God wants to help us grow and succeed. When things are difficult, remember that His plans are filled with hope and a bright future. Take a moment each day to pray and ask Him to show you the way. Trusting in His plan will help you feel stronger and more at peace!

DAILY REFLECTION

Think about a time when you felt unsure about what to do next. How can remembering that God has a special plan for you help you feel more hopeful and confident in those moments? Take a moment to write down your thoughts and any prayers you want to share with God about your journey.

PRAYER

Dear God, thank you for the special plan you have for each of us, filled with hope and a bright future. When we feel lost or unsure, help us to trust in Your guidance, knowing that You are always with us, showing the way to grow and succeed.

WHEN YOU FEEL SPIRITUALLY DRY

"For I will pour water on the thirsty land, and streams on the dry ground; I will pour out my Spirit on your offspring, and my blessing on your descendants." Isaiah 44:3

DEVOTIONAL

Sometimes, we may feel spiritually dry, like a plant in need of rain. Remember, God promises to pour His Spirit like water on thirsty land. When you feel empty, take a moment to pray, read your Bible, or sing a song of praise. These are ways God refreshes us. Just as streams nourish the ground, God fills our hearts with His love and blessings. Trust Him to renew your spirit today and always.

DAILY REFLECTION

Think about a time when you felt a bit empty or lacking energy. What is one thing you can do today to invite God's love and blessings into your heart?

PRAYER

Dear God, thank you for always being there to fill our hearts with Your love, especially when we feel a little empty inside. Help us to remember to pray, read Your Word, or sing our favorite songs, so we can feel Your refreshing Spirit and be renewed by Your blessings.

GOD IS IN THE DETAILS

"Look at the birds of the air; they do not sow or reap or store away in barns, and yet your heavenly Father feeds them. Are you not much more valuable than they?" Matthew 6:26

DEVOTIONAL

God cares for every tiny detail in our lives, just like He cares for the birds. Matthew 6:26 reminds us that if He provides for the birds, He will surely take care of us! When you see a bird flying or singing, remember that God loves you even more. He knows what you need and is always watching over you. Trust Him with your worries, and notice the little blessings around you—God is in the details!

DAILY REFLECTION

Think about a time when you noticed something small, like a bird singing or a flower blooming. How did that moment remind you of God's care for you? Take a moment to write down how you can trust Him with your worries and appreciate the little blessings in your life today.

PRAYER

Dear God, thank you for caring about every little part of our lives, just like you take care of the birds and the flowers. Help us to trust you with our worries and to see the beautiful blessings you give us each day, reminding us of your endless love.

LETTING GO OF THE PAST

"Forget the former things; do not dwell on the past." Isaiah 43:18

DEVOTIONAL

Sometimes, we hold on to things that make us sad or worried, like mistakes or hurts from the past. But in Isaiah 43:18, God tells us to let those things go! When we let go, we make room for the new blessings God has for us. Each day is a fresh start, filled with God's love and promise. Trust Him to help you move forward, leaving the past behind and embracing a brighter, joyful future.

DAILY REFLECTION

What is one thing from your past that you find it hard to let go of, and how can you take a small step today to release it and make space for something new in your life?

PRAYER

Dear God, help me to let go of the things that make me sad or worried, and remind me that each day is a fresh start filled with Your love. As I take small steps to release my burdens, open my heart to the new blessings You have in store for me.

CHOOSING FAITH IN UNCERTAINTY

"Trust in the Lord with all your heart and lean not on your own understanding."
Proverbs 3:5

DEVOTIONAL

When life feels uncertain, it's easy to worry. But God wants us to trust Him fully! Proverbs 3:5 reminds us to lean on Him instead of our own understanding. Imagine you're walking in a dark room and can't see where to go. Just like a friend guiding you, God leads you with His love. When you choose faith, you open your heart to His plans. Today, let go of your worries and trust that God is with you every step!

DAILY REFLECTION

When you think about a time when you felt uncertain or worried, how did you respond? What does trusting God look like for you in those moments?

PRAYER

Dear God, when I feel uncertain and worried, help me to remember that You are always with me, guiding me with Your love. Teach me to trust in Your plans and let go of my fears, knowing that You will lead me safely through every dark moment.

YOU ARE SEEN AND KNOWN

"You know when I sit and when I rise; you perceive my thoughts from afar." Psalm 139:2

DEVOTIONAL

God knows you inside and out—every thought, every feeling, every moment. When you sit quietly or jump with joy, He sees you. This is a wonderful reminder that you are never alone. God cares about what you're going through and celebrates your joys. Remember, you can always turn to Him in prayer, sharing your heart. Embrace this truth today: you are seen and known by the Creator of the universe, who loves you just as you are.

DAILY REFLECTION

How does knowing that God knows everything about you make you feel about the things happening in your life right now? Take a moment to think about a joy you have or a struggle you are facing and consider how you can talk to God about it in prayer.

PRAYER

Dear God, thank you for knowing me completely, from my joys to my struggles, and for always being here to listen. Help me remember that I am never alone, and guide me as I share my heart with you in prayer.

THE STRENGTH OF QUIET OBEDIENCE

"For the LORD your God is with you wherever you go." Joshua 1:9

DEVOTIONAL

In our busy lives, it's easy to feel lost and unsure. Yet, God promises, "For the LORD your God is with you wherever you go" (Joshua 1:9). This means we can find strength in quiet obedience, trusting Him with our choices. When we listen to God's guidance and follow His way, we grow closer to Him. Each small act of faith, like helping a friend or being honest, shows our love for God. Let's embrace His presence today!

DAILY REFLECTION

Reflect on a recent moment when you felt unsure or lost. How can you invite God's presence into that situation, and what small act of faith can you choose today to show your trust in Him?

PRAYER

Dear God, thank you for always being with us, even when we feel lost or unsure. Help us to trust in Your guidance and to show our love for You through small acts of kindness today.

REFINED BY FIRE

"When you pass through the waters, I will be with you; and when you pass through the rivers, they will not sweep over you." Isaiah 43:2

DEVOTIONAL

Life can sometimes feel like a tough fire, but remember, God is right there with you! Isaiah 43:2 tells us that when we face challenges, we won't be overwhelmed; He protects us like a warm blanket in a storm. These moments help us grow stronger in our faith. So, when things get hard, take a deep breath and talk to God. Trust that He's using these struggles to make you better, just like gold is refined by fire.

DAILY REFLECTION

Think about a challenging moment you've faced recently. How did you feel in that situation, and how did you remind yourself that God was with you? Take a moment to reflect on how this experience has helped you grow in your faith. What insights or lessons can you take forward with you?

PRAYER

Dear God, thank you for being with me during tough times, just like a warm blanket that keeps me safe. Help me to remember that every challenge I face is a chance to grow stronger in my faith and trust in Your love.

GOD'S GRACE IN YOUR WEAKNESS

"My grace is sufficient for you, for my power is made perfect in weakness." 2 Corinthians 12:9

DEVOTIONAL

When we feel weak or unsure, remember God's promise: His grace is enough! In 2 Corinthians 12:9, He tells us that His strength shines brightest when we have struggles. Think about a time you felt weak—maybe when learning something new or facing a challenge. That's when God helps us the most! Embrace your weaknesses, for they open a door for God's love and power to lift you. Trust Him, and you will grow stronger in faith.

DAILY REFLECTION

Reflect on a moment in your life when you faced a challenge that made you feel weak or unsure. How did that experience help you notice God's strength and grace in your life? What did you learn about trusting Him during that time?

PRAYER

Dear God, thank you for being with us when we feel weak or uncertain; help us to remember that Your grace is always enough to lift us up. May we find strength in our struggles and trust in Your love, knowing that every challenge is an opportunity for Your power to shine through us.

LIVING INTENTIONALLY

"Whatever you do, work heartily, as for the Lord and not for men." Colossians 3:23

DEVOTIONAL

Every day is a chance to make our actions count! In Colossians 3:23, we are reminded to work heartily, as if we're doing it for God. This means that whether we're doing chores, helping a friend, or studying, we can choose to do our best. Living intentionally means bringing our best to everything, showing love and care in our actions. Let's remember that God is always watching, and every effort we make is for Him.

DAILY REFLECTION

Think about a time today when you did something, like helping someone or working on a task. How did you try to show your best in that moment, and how did it make you feel to know you were doing it for God?

PRAYER

Dear God, thank you for each new day and the opportunity to show love through our actions. Help us to remember that every time we work hard or offer a helping hand, we are doing it for You, and let that fill our hearts with joy and purpose.

THE JOY OF THE LORD IS YOUR STRENGTH

"The joy of the Lord is your strength." Nehemiah 8:10

DEVOTIONAL

The joy of the Lord is your strength, which means that happiness from God can help you through tough times. When we remember God's love and goodness, it fills our hearts with joy. This joy helps us be brave and face challenges with a smile. Whenever you feel sad or tired, take a moment to pray and thank God for the good things in your life. Let His joy lift you up and give you the strength you need!

DAILY REFLECTION

Reflect on a time when you felt sad or tired. What good things in your life could you thank God for to help lift your spirits? How can remembering His love and joy help you face challenges in the future?

PRAYER

Dear God, thank you for the joy you give us that makes our hearts feel light even when times are tough. Help us to remember all the good things in our lives and feel your love, so we can be brave and face any challenge with a smile.

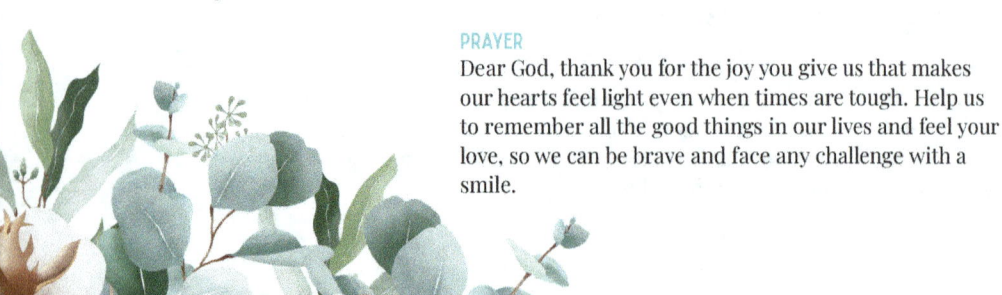

CLINGING TO WHAT IS GOOD

"Hold on to what is good, cling to what is good." 1 Thessalonians 5:21

DEVOTIONAL

In 1 Thessalonians 5:21, we are reminded to hold on to what is good. Think of all the beautiful things in your life—like love, kindness, and joy. God wants us to cherish these treasures. Each day, find ways to show love and share kindness; this makes our hearts grow closer to Him. Remember, even during tough times, clinging to what is good helps us see God's light. Let your heart be a home for all that is good!

DAILY REFLECTION

Reflect on the beautiful things in your life. What are three things that bring you joy or make you feel loved? How can you share that joy or love with someone else today?

PRAYER

Dear God, thank you for the beautiful things in my life that fill my heart with joy and love, like my family, friends, and the kindness I see around me. Help me to treasure these gifts and share their light with others, so that we may all grow closer to You. Amen.

FAITHFUL IN THE SMALL THINGS

"And he said to him, 'Well done, good servant! Because you were faithful in a very little, you shall be in charge of much.'" Luke 19:17

DEVOTIONAL

In Luke 19:17, Jesus praises the servant for being faithful in small tasks. This reminds us that even little things matter to God. When we help others, share our toys, or say kind words, we are showing faithfulness. Each small action pleases God and prepares us for bigger responsibilities. Remember, no act of kindness is too small! Let's be faithful in our daily tasks, trusting that God sees all we do and will reward us in His perfect time.

DAILY REFLECTION

What is one small act of kindness you can do today that shows your faithfulness to God and helps someone else?

PRAYER

Dear God, thank you for reminding us that small acts of kindness matter to You. Help us to share, help, and care for others today, knowing that each little thing we do shows our love and faithfulness to You.

RENEWING YOUR MIND

"Do not conform to the pattern of this world, but be transformed by the renewing of your mind." Romans 12:2

DEVOTIONAL

Every day, our minds are filled with thoughts from the world around us. Romans 12:2 reminds us not to fit into those patterns. Instead, we can let God change our thinking. This means choosing to fill our minds with His words and love. When we do, we see the world differently—filled with hope and joy. Let's take a moment each day to read the Bible and pray, allowing God to renew our minds and grow our hearts in faith.

DAILY REFLECTION

What is one thought or worry you can give to God today, and how might focusing on His words change the way you see your situation?

PRAYER

Dear God, thank you for reminding us that we can choose to fill our minds with Your love and words instead of the worries around us. Help us to trust in You, seek your guidance, and see our world with hope and joy as we grow in faith.

THE BEAUTY OF SURRENDER

"Trust in the Lord with all your heart and lean not on your own understanding." Proverbs 3:5

DEVOTIONAL

Surrendering to God means trusting Him completely, even when things are confusing or scary. Proverbs 3:5 tells us to trust in the Lord with all our hearts and not rely on what we think we know. When we let go of our worries and fears, we allow God to guide us in His perfect plan. Surrender brings peace and helps us grow closer to Him. Remember, God loves you and always knows what's best for you!

DAILY REFLECTION

Reflect on a time when you felt confused or scared about something happening in your life. What worries were weighing on your heart? How can you practice surrendering those feelings to God, trusting that He has a plan for you? Consider what it might look like to let go of those worries and lean on Him for guidance.

PRAYER

Dear God, I thank you for always being with me, even when I feel scared or confused. Help me to trust you with my worries and to remember that you have a perfect plan for my life, bringing me peace as I lean on your love and guidance.

HE WORKS ALL THINGS FOR GOOD

"And we know that in all things God works for the good of those who love him, who have been called according to his purpose." Romans 8:28

DEVOTIONAL

God has a special plan for you! Romans 8:28 reminds us that He works in every situation to bring good to those who love Him. Even when things seem tough or confusing, trust that God is there, guiding you. Take a moment to reflect on a challenge you're facing. Ask God to help you see how He is working through it. Remember, every twist and turn in your life can lead you closer to Him and His purpose for you.

DAILY REFLECTION

Reflect on a challenge you're currently facing. How can you invite God into this situation and trust that He is working for your good? Take a moment to think about what guidance you might ask from Him and how this experience could help you grow closer to His purpose for your life.

PRAYER

Dear God, thank you for loving me and for your special plan in my life. Please help me to trust you when things feel hard and to see how you are working for my good in every situation.

A STEADFAST SPIRIT

"Create in me a clean heart, O God, and renew a steadfast spirit within me." Psalm 51:10

DEVOTIONAL

In Psalm 51:10, we learn about the importance of having a clean heart and a steadfast spirit. A steadfast spirit means being strong and faithful, even when things are tough. We can ask God to help us stay focused on Him and make good choices every day. Remember, God loves us and wants to guide us. Let's pray for a heart full of love and a spirit that never gives up, trusting in His promises.

DAILY REFLECTION

Reflect on a time when you faced a challenge and had to make a difficult choice. How did you rely on your faith to help you stay strong and focused? What did you learn about having a clean heart and a steadfast spirit from that experience?

PRAYER

Dear God, please help us to have clean hearts full of love and steadfast spirits that stay strong when challenges come our way. Guide us to make good choices each day, trusting in Your love and promises, knowing You are always with us.

HOPE THAT HOLDS

"May the God of hope fill you with all joy and peace as you trust in him, so that you may overflow with hope by the power of the Holy Spirit." Romans 15:13

DEVOTIONAL

Hope is like a bright light in a dark room, guiding us when things feel tough. Romans 15:13 reminds us that God wants to fill our hearts with joy and peace as we trust in Him. When we lean on God, His Holy Spirit helps us overflow with hope. This hope is a gift we can share with others. Today, let's trust God and let His hope shine through us, bringing joy to our hearts and those around us.

DAILY REFLECTION

How can you be a source of hope for someone else today, and in what ways can you trust God to shine His light through you?

PRAYER

Dear God, thank you for the bright light of hope that guides us when times are tough. Help us to share this hope with others, trusting in Your love to shine through us and bring joy to our hearts and the hearts of those around us.

CASTING YOUR CARES

"Cast all your anxiety on him because he cares for you." 1 Peter 5:7

DEVOTIONAL

When we feel worried or scared, it's easy to get overwhelmed. But in 1 Peter 5:7, God reminds us to give those heavy feelings to Him. Imagine standing by a stream, tossing pebbles into the water. Each pebble represents a worry. As you let them go, feel the peace wash over you. God loves you and wants to help! Remember, you don't have to carry your worries alone. Trust Him and let His love lift you up every day.

DAILY REFLECTION

Reflect on a time when you felt worried or scared. What are some "pebbles" of worry you can let go of today? How can you feel God's love and peace as you release those worries?

PRAYER

Dear God, when worries and fears feel too heavy, help us to find comfort in Your love as we release them like pebbles into a gentle stream. Thank You for reminding us that we don't have to carry these burdens alone, and may Your peace wash over us as we trust in You.

HE IS WITH YOU ALWAYS
"And surely I am with you always, to the very end of the age." Matthew 28:20

DEVOTIONAL
In Matthew 28:20, Jesus promises, "I am with you always." This means, no matter where you are—at school, home, or with friends—God is right beside you, watching over you. When you feel scared or alone, remember that He is there to comfort and guide you. Take a moment each day to talk to Him. Share your worries and joys. By inviting God into every moment, you'll feel His presence and grow closer to Him each day.

DAILY REFLECTION
How can you invite God into your daily activities, and what are some specific moments when you might feel His presence during your day?

PRAYER
Dear God, thank you for always being with me, just like you promised, no matter where I am or what I'm feeling. Help me to talk to you in everything I do, so I can feel your love and guidance each day as I share my worries and joys.

WALKING IN THE LIGHT
"Walk in the light as He is in the light." 1 John 1:7

DEVOTIONAL
Walking in the light means following Jesus and letting His goodness shine in our lives. When we choose to do what is right and love others, we reflect His light to the world. Just like a flashlight helps us see in the dark, Jesus helps us make good choices. Each day, let's remember to share kindness and joy, showing others the light of God through our actions. As we walk in His light, we grow closer to Him.

DAILY REFLECTION
How can you choose to show kindness and love to someone today, and in what way do you feel that will help you reflect Jesus' light in the world?

PRAYER
Dear God, help us to walk in Your light and let our actions shine with kindness and love, just like Jesus shows us. May we reflect Your goodness to others today, making the world brighter with our caring hearts.

FORGIVENESS IS FREEDOM

"Therefore, if the Son makes you free, you shall be free indeed." John 8:36

DEVOTIONAL

Forgiveness is like a key that unlocks a cage. When we hold onto anger or hurt, we feel trapped. But when we choose to forgive, we set ourselves free! Jesus tells us in John 8:36 that He gives us true freedom. This means letting go of what others have done to us and welcoming peace into our hearts. Today, think of someone you can forgive. Remember, forgiveness helps us grow closer to God and find joy in His love.

DAILY REFLECTION

Think about a time when someone hurt you or made you feel angry. How can choosing to forgive that person help you feel free and closer to God? Share your thoughts in a journal or with a friend.

PRAYER

Dear God, thank you for teaching us about forgiveness and the freedom it brings. Help us to let go of our anger and open our hearts to peace, so we may grow closer to You and fill our lives with joy.

BEARING SPIRITUAL FRUIT

"But the fruit of the Spirit is love, joy, peace, forbearance, kindness, goodness, faithfulness, gentleness and self-control." Galatians 5:22-23

DEVOTIONAL

God gives us special gifts called the fruits of the Spirit. In Galatians 5:22-23, we learn that these fruits are love, joy, peace, forbearance, kindness, goodness, faithfulness, gentleness, and self-control. Each day, we can ask God to help us grow in these areas. When we show love, spread joy, and offer kindness, we not only grow closer to God but also shine His light to others. Let's practice bearing good fruit and make the world brighter!

DAILY REFLECTION

How can you demonstrate one of the fruits of the Spirit, like kindness or joy, to someone in your life this week? Think about a small way you can show this fruit and how it might make a difference for them.

PRAYER

Dear God, thank you for the beautiful gifts of love, joy, and kindness that help us shine Your light in the world. Please guide us this week to grow in these fruits of the Spirit and show them to others, making our hearts and those around us brighter.

THE PEACE OF LETTING GO

"Cast all your anxiety on him because he cares for you." 1 Peter 5:7

DEVOTIONAL

When worries fill your mind, remember 1 Peter 5:7: "Cast all your anxiety on him because he cares for you." God wants to help you! Imagine tossing a heavy backpack filled with rocks far away. Just like that, give your anxieties to God. He is gentle and loving, ready to take your burdens. Whenever you feel anxious, take a deep breath and talk to Him. You'll find peace and comfort in knowing He cares for you deeply.

DAILY REFLECTION

When you feel anxious or worried, how can you practice letting go of those feelings and trust that God is there to help you? Think about a time you can visualize giving your worries to Him. What does that look like for you?

PRAYER

Dear God, help me to let go of my worries and trust that you are always with me, holding me close. Thank you for caring for my heart and bringing me peace when I release my burdens to you.

STRENGTH TO BEGIN AGAIN

"Forget the former things; do not dwell on the past. See, I am doing a new thing!" Isaiah 43:18-19

DEVOTIONAL

Sometimes, it's easy to feel stuck in our past mistakes or worries. But in Isaiah 43:18-19, God reminds us to let go of what's behind us. He is always working to make things new! Just like seasons change, we can start fresh each day. This is a chance to grow closer to God, discovering new strengths and joys. When you feel weighed down, remember that God is with you, helping you begin again. Trust Him!

DAILY REFLECTION

As you prepare for this new season, take a moment to think about something from your past that you feel stuck on. How can you let go of that worry or mistake, and what new strength or joy do you hope to discover as you trust in God to help you begin again?

PRAYER

Dear God, thank you for always being with us, helping us to let go of our past worries and mistakes. Please guide us as we embrace new beginnings, discovering joyful moments and strengths in our hearts each day.

YOUR LIFE IS A TESTIMONY

Let your light shine before others, that they may see your good deeds and glorify your Father in heaven. Matthew 5:16

DEVOTIONAL

Your life tells a story that others can see! When you choose to be kind, helpful, or loving, you shine a light that shows God's love to the world. Just like a candle brightens a dark room, your good deeds help others learn about God. Remember, every time you share joy or do something nice, you reflect His goodness. Let your actions inspire others to find Him, and let your light shine brightly for all to see!

DAILY REFLECTION

As you think about your day, consider this: What is one kind action you can take today that would show others God's love? How might that action brighten someone else's day and inspire them to share love too?

PRAYER

Dear God, thank you for the light of Your love that shines through us when we choose to be kind and helpful. Help us to find small ways to show kindness today, so that others can feel Your love and joy through our actions.

RESTORING JOY

"Restore to me the joy of your salvation, and uphold me with a willing spirit." Psalm 51:12

DEVOTIONAL

Sometimes, we might feel sad or lose our joy. In Psalm 51:12, David asks God to bring back the happiness that comes from knowing Him. When we remember how much God loves us and the gift of salvation, our hearts can be filled with joy again. Take a moment today to talk to God about how you feel. Ask Him to help you see His love and to fill your spirit with joy. Trust that He will!

DAILY REFLECTION

Reflect on a time when you felt sad or lost your joy. What is one way you can remember God's love and salvation in that moment? Take a few minutes to talk to God about how you feel and ask Him to fill your heart with joy again. What do you hope to feel or see as you do this?

PRAYER

Dear God, thank You for loving me no matter how I feel. Please fill my heart with Your joy and help me remember how special Your love is, so I can feel happy again.

GOD'S POWER IN YOUR STORY

"For the Spirit God gave us does not make us timid, but gives us power, love, and self-discipline." 2 Timothy 1:7

DEVOTIONAL

God has a special purpose for your life, and He is powerful enough to help you discover it! In 2 Timothy 1:7, we learn that God does not make us shy; instead, He gives us strength, love, and self-control. When you feel afraid or unsure, remember that you can ask God for help. His power can turn your fears into courage and your doubts into faith. Trust Him to lead your story with love and strength!

DAILY REFLECTION

When you think about your dreams and what you'd like to achieve, how can you remind yourself that God is there to give you strength and courage when you feel uncertain?

PRAYER

Dear God, thank you for your wonderful plan for my life and for giving me strength, love, and the courage to follow my dreams. When I feel unsure or scared, help me to trust in your power and remember that you are always by my side, guiding me with your love.

ENDURING WITH GRACE

"But he said to me, 'My grace is sufficient for you, for my power is made perfect in weakness.'" 2 Corinthians 12:9

DEVOTIONAL

When we feel weak or face tough times, it can be hard to keep going. But remember, God tells us that His grace is enough for us! This means that even when we struggle, His love and strength help us through. Just like a flower grows stronger in the rain, our faith grows when we lean on God. So, when challenges come, trust that God's grace will lift you up and give you the power to endure.

DAILY REFLECTION

When you face challenges and feel weak, how can you remember to lean on God's grace for strength? What are some ways you can show your trust in Him during tough times?

PRAYER

Dear God, thank you for your endless love and strength, especially when we feel weak or face tough times. Help us to trust in Your grace and remember that You are always with us, guiding us through every challenge we encounter.

PREPARING FOR A NEW SEASON

"Behold, I am doing a new thing; now it springs forth, do you not perceive it?" Isaiah 43:19

DEVOTIONAL

As we step into a new season, remember that God is always at work in our lives. Isaiah 43:19 reminds us that He is doing something new, even when we can't see it. Just like the trees change with the seasons, we too can grow and change. Let's be open to God's surprises, praying for courage to embrace His plans. This season can be a time to learn, grow, and trust in His good purpose for us.

DAILY REFLECTION

As you think about the changes happening in your life right now, what is one new thing you can embrace this season, and how can you open your heart to see God's work in it?

PRAYER

Dear God, thank You for always working in our lives, even when we can't see what You're doing. Help us to be brave and open our hearts to the new things You have for us this season, trusting that You are guiding us on a beautiful journey of growth and change.

ENTERING A NEW SEASON WITH FAITH

"Behold, I am doing a new thing; now it springs forth, do you not perceive it?"
Isaiah 43:19

DEVOTIONAL

As we enter a new season, remember God's promise in Isaiah 43:19: "Behold, I am doing a new thing!" Change can feel scary, but it's also a chance for growth. Just like flowers bloom in spring, God is inviting us to blossom in our faith. Look for the good things He is doing around you. Pray for understanding and trust Him to guide your steps. Embrace this new chapter, knowing God is with you every step of the way.

DAILY REFLECTION

As you reflect on the idea that God is doing a new thing in your life, what are some areas where you feel challenged by change, and how can you trust God to help you grow through these experiences?

PRAYER

Dear God, as we embrace this new season, help us to see the beauty in change and trust that you are guiding our steps. May we blossom in our faith and recognize the good things you are doing in our lives, even when things feel uncertain.

RESTING IN GOD'S RHYTHM

"Come to me, all you who are weary and burdened, and I will give you rest."
Matthew 11:28

DEVOTIONAL

Life can feel busy and overwhelming, just like a race. But God invites us to step back and rest in His rhythm. In Matthew 11:28, He promises to give us rest when we come to Him. Picture a peaceful stream where you can find calmness. Take time today to talk to God about your worries and ask for His help. Remember, resting in Him means trusting that He will guide you through every challenge. Embrace His peace!

DAILY REFLECTION

As you think about the busyness of your life, what worries are weighing on your mind right now? How can you take a moment to rest in God's presence and trust that He will guide you through these challenges?

PRAYER

As you think about the busyness of your life, what worries are weighing on your mind right now? How can you take a moment to rest in God's presence and trust that He will guide you through these challenges?

WHEN YOU FEEL BEHIND

"But those who hope in the Lord will renew their strength." Isaiah 40:31

DEVOTIONAL

When you feel behind, remember Isaiah 40:31: "But those who hope in the Lord will renew their strength." Sometimes, life can feel overwhelming, and we worry about keeping up. But God is always there to help us. When we turn to Him in prayer and trust Him, He fills us with strength and courage. Instead of focusing on what you haven't done, rest in His love, and let His joy carry you forward. Keep hoping in Him!

DAILY REFLECTION

Think about a time when you felt behind or overwhelmed. How did you turn to God for help during that time? What is one way you can remind yourself to hope in Him the next time you feel this way?

PRAYER

Dear God, when I feel behind or overwhelmed, help me to remember that I can always turn to You for strength and courage. Fill my heart with Your love, guiding me to hope in You so that I can rise above my worries and find joy in each day.

SEEKING GOD FIRST

"But seek first the kingdom of God and his righteousness, and all these things will be added to you." Matthew 6:33

DEVOTIONAL

Every day is a chance to make choices. In Matthew 6:33, Jesus reminds us to seek God first. This means putting Him at the center of our hearts and decisions. When we focus on loving God and doing what is right, He takes care of our needs. Trust that as you seek Him—through prayer, reading the Bible, and helping others—He will bless you with everything you need. Remember, God is always with you, guiding your path.

DAILY REFLECTION

As you think about your daily choices, how can you make sure to put God at the center of your decisions today? Consider one specific action you can take to seek Him first in your life.

PRAYER

Dear God, thank You for the gift of today and for the choices we can make to love and follow You. Help us to always put You at the center of our hearts, guiding our decisions with Your wisdom and love.

YOU ARE NEVER ALONE

"For I am with you, and no one will attack you to harm you, for I have many in this city who are my people." Acts 18:10

DEVOTIONAL

In life, you may sometimes feel lonely or scared, but remember that God is always with you. Just like He told Paul in Acts 18:10, He promises to be by your side and to protect you. You're part of a bigger family of believers who also love and support you. When you feel uncertain, talk to God. He listens and cares. Trust that you are never truly alone; His presence is always with you, guiding you each day.

DAILY REFLECTION

Think about a time when you felt lonely or scared. How did you find comfort in knowing that God is with you? What can you do this week to remind yourself of His presence and the support of your bigger family in faith?

PRAYER

Dear God, thank You for always being by my side, especially when I feel lonely or scared. Help me to remember Your love and the support of my faith family, so I can find comfort and courage in You each day.

REFRESHED BY HIS PRESENCE

"Restore to me the joy of your salvation, and grant me a willing spirit, to sustain me." Psalm 51:12

DEVOTIONAL

Sometimes, we can feel tired or sad, but spending time with God can refresh us! In Psalm 51:12, David asks God to restore his joy and help him. When we pray and read the Bible, God fills our hearts with happiness and strength. Remember, it's okay to ask Him to renew your spirit! This week, find a quiet moment to sit with God. Let His presence lift you up and remind you of His love!

DAILY REFLECTION

Think about a time when you felt tired or sad. How did spending time with God help you feel better or lift your spirits? What is one thing you can do this week to create a quiet moment with Him?

PRAYER

Dear God, thank you for being a loving friend who lifts our spirits when we feel tired or sad. Please help us to find quiet moments this week to spend with You, so we can feel Your joy and strength in our hearts.

TRUSTING GOD'S BIGGER PICTURE

"For I know the plans I have for you," declares the Lord, "plans to prosper you and not to harm you, plans to give you hope and a future." Jeremiah 29:11

DEVOTIONAL

Sometimes, life feels confusing and we can't see what's ahead. But God promises that He has a special plan just for you (Jeremiah 29:11). Think about a puzzle: all the pieces seem scattered, but when you trust the process, the picture comes together. Today, remember that God sees the bigger picture and is working for your good. Even when things seem tough, trust that He's guiding you towards hope and a bright future filled with His love.

DAILY REFLECTION

Think about a time when you felt confused or unsure about what was happening in your life. Can you remember how you felt? Now, reflect on how trusting in God's plan helped you find hope or comfort in that situation. How can you remind yourself to trust in His guidance when things feel scattered, like a puzzle waiting to be put together?

PRAYER

Dear God, thank you for the promise that you have a special plan for each of us, even when life feels confusing, like a puzzle with scattered pieces. Help us to trust in your guidance and remember that you see the bigger picture, leading us toward hope and love.

THE FRUIT OF THE SPIRIT

"But the fruit of the Spirit is love, joy, peace, forbearance, kindness, goodness, faithfulness, gentleness and self-control." Galatians 5:22-23

DEVOTIONAL

The Fruit of the Spirit helps us grow closer to God and to others. Imagine planting a seed that turns into a tree full of delicious fruit! When we have love, joy, and peace, we shine brightly for Jesus. Each day, we can practice kindness and patience, showing goodness and faithfulness in our actions. As we learn to be gentle and have self-control, we become more like Jesus. Let's ask God to help us grow this fruit in our hearts!

DAILY REFLECTION

How can you practice one of the Fruits of the Spirit—like kindness or patience —today to help yourself grow closer to God and share His love with others?

PRAYER

Dear God, thank You for teaching us about the wonderful Fruit of the Spirit, which helps us grow closer to You and to each other. Please help us to practice kindness and patience every day, so we can shine brightly for Jesus and share Your love with everyone around us.

A FAITH THAT GROWS

"But grow in the grace and knowledge of our Lord and Savior Jesus Christ." 2 Peter 3:18

DEVOTIONAL

As we grow taller, our faith can grow too! Just like a plant needs sunlight and water, our faith needs love and knowledge of Jesus. When we read the Bible and pray, we're giving our faith what it needs to thrive. Every day is a chance to learn something new about God and to show His love to others. Remember, the more we learn about Jesus, the stronger our faith becomes. Let's keep growing together!

DAILY REFLECTION

How can you take a small step today to learn more about Jesus and show His love to someone around you?

PRAYER

Dear God, thank you for helping us grow in faith just like flowers reach for the sun. Please guide us as we learn more about Jesus and remind us to share His love with everyone around us.

FINDING JOY IN SERVING

"For even the Son of Man did not come to be served, but to serve, and to give His life as a ransom for many." Mark 10:45

DEVOTIONAL

When we think about Jesus, we remember how much He loved to help others. In Mark 10:45, it tells us that Jesus came to serve, not to be served. Serving others, like showing kindness or helping a friend, can bring us great joy! When we share our time and talents, we shine God's love. Each act of kindness can bring us closer to Jesus. Let's find joy in serving, just like He did, and watch how it changes our hearts!

DAILY REFLECTION

How can you show kindness to someone today, and how do you think that act of service might help you feel closer to Jesus?

PRAYER

Dear Jesus, thank You for showing us how to love and serve others with joy. Help us to find ways to share kindness today, so that we can feel closer to You and shine Your love in the world.

GOD IS YOUR SHELTER

"He who dwells in the secret place of the Most High shall abide under the shadow of the Almighty." Psalm 91:1

DEVOTIONAL

God is like a cozy shelter where we can feel safe and loved. When we spend time with Him, praying or reading the Bible, we find comfort under His care. Psalm 91:1 reminds us that if we stay close to God, He protects us, like a strong shadow on a sunny day. Remember, no matter what worries you face, you can always run to Him for help. Trust in His love and let Him be your safe place.

DAILY REFLECTION

How can you create quiet moments in your day to spend time with God, allowing His love and protection to comfort you?

PRAYER

Dear God, thank you for being our cozy shelter where we feel safe and loved, like a warm hug on a sunny day. Help us to remember to pause and spend quiet moments with You, trusting in Your love to guide and protect us always.

THE POWER OF YOUR WORDS

"Death and life are in the power of the tongue, and those who love it will eat its fruits." Proverbs 18:21

DEVOTIONAL

Our words are very powerful! The Bible tells us that they can bring life or cause hurt. When we speak kindly and lovingly, we help others feel happy and valued. Just like a garden, our words grow good things when we choose them wisely. This week, let's focus on lifting people up with our words and sharing God's love. Remember, what we say can be a blessing! Choose to speak life and watch how it changes your world.

DAILY REFLECTION

How can you use your words this week to encourage someone and make them feel valued? Think of a specific person you can uplift with your kind words and what you might say to them.

PRAYER

How can you use your words this week to encourage someone and make them feel valued? Think of a specific person you can uplift with your kind words and what you might say to them.

RETURNING TO GOD'S HEART

"Draw near to God, and He will draw near to you." James 4:8

DEVOTIONAL

When we feel far from God, it's often because we've wandered away. James 4:8 reminds us that if we take a step toward Him, He will come closer to us. Think of every prayer, kind act, and moment spent in the Bible as a way to draw near to His heart. Just like a warm hug, God's love welcomes us back. Each day is a chance to grow in faith and feel His presence surrounding us.

DAILY REFLECTION

Reflect on a time when you felt distant from God. What steps can you take today—through prayer, kindness, or reading the Bible—to draw closer to Him? Consider how these actions can help you feel His presence in your life.

PRAYER

Dear God, thank you for always welcoming us back with open arms, even when we feel distant. Help us to take small steps toward You today through prayer, kindness, and reading Your Word, so we can feel Your love surround us like a warm hug.

EVERY SEASON HAS PURPOSE

"For everything there is a season, and a time for every matter under heaven." Ecclesiastes 3:1

DEVOTIONAL

Every season in our lives has a special purpose, just like the changing seasons outside. God's Word in Ecclesiastes 3:1 reminds us that there is a time for everything. In spring, we see new beginnings; in summer, we enjoy warmth and growth. Autumn teaches us to let go, while winter invites us to rest. Trust that God is with you in every season, guiding you to learn and grow closer to Him. Embrace each moment!

DAILY REFLECTION

Think about a season in your life that you are currently experiencing. What lessons do you believe God is teaching you during this time, and how can you embrace this season to grow closer to Him?

PRAYER

Dear God, thank you for the beautiful seasons in our lives, each one teaching us valuable lessons and drawing us closer to You. Help us to embrace our current season with open hearts, trusting in Your guidance and love as we grow and learn each day.

LIVING WITH SPIRITUAL CLARITY

"Seek the Lord and His strength; seek His presence continually." 1 Chronicles 16:11

DEVOTIONAL

Living with spiritual clarity means turning our hearts to God every day. When we seek Him, as it says in 1 Chronicles 16:11, we find strength and comfort. Think of God as a flashlight that guides you through dark paths and helps you see clearly. Spending time in prayer and reading the Bible helps us know Him better. Remember, He is always with you, ready to help when you call on Him. Keep seeking, and watch your faith grow!

DAILY REFLECTION

As you think about how turning your heart to God can guide you like a flashlight, what are some ways you can seek Him today? Consider how spending time in prayer or reading the Bible might help you feel His presence and strengthen your faith.

PRAYER

Dear God, help me to turn my heart towards You every day, just like a flashlight guiding me through dark paths. As I spend time in prayer and read Your word, may I feel Your love and strength, growing my faith and understanding of Your presence in my life.

LETTING GOD CARRY THE LOAD

"Cast all your anxiety on him because he cares for you." 1 Peter 5:7

DEVOTIONAL

Sometimes, life feels heavy, and we carry worries and fears on our shoulders. But God tells us to give Him those burdens. In 1 Peter 5:7, we learn that we can "cast all our anxiety on Him." This means we can share our worries with God, trusting He cares for us deeply. When we let God carry our load, we find peace and comfort. Today, take a moment to tell Him what's on your heart and let Him help you.

DAILY REFLECTION

Reflect on a worry or fear that has been heavy on your heart. What does it feel like to imagine giving that concern to God? How can you trust Him to help you carry this burden? Take a moment to express your feelings and thoughts to Him. What peace do you find in knowing you are not alone in handling this?

PRAYER

Dear God, thank You for reminding me that I don't have to carry my worries alone; I can share my fears with You and trust that You care deeply for me. Help me to lay my heavy thoughts at Your feet, and fill my heart with peace, knowing that You are always with me, ready to help and guide me.

HOPE IN THE HIDDEN PLACES

"Behold, I will do a new thing; now it shall spring forth; shall you not know it? I will even make a road in the wilderness and rivers in the desert." Isaiah 43:19

DEVOTIONAL

In life, we sometimes feel lost, like we're wandering through a wilderness where hope seems hidden. Isaiah 43:19 reminds us that God is always at work, bringing new beginnings even when we can't see them. Just as He can create a path in the wilderness and rivers in the dry desert, He can bring hope to our lives. Trust in Him, for He brings joy and new growth, even in the hardest times. Let's look for His surprises today!

DAILY REFLECTION

Reflect on a time when you felt lost or unsure in your own life. How did you recognize God's presence or guidance in that situation? What new beginnings or surprises did you discover after that experience? Take a moment to think about how you can trust in Him during challenging times and look for His work in your life today.

PRAYER

Dear God, when we feel lost and unsure, help us to remember that You are always with us, creating new paths and bringing hope from the hidden places. May we trust in Your loving guidance and be open to the beautiful surprises You have in store for our lives.

OBEDIENT IN THE UNKNOWN

"Trust in the Lord with all your heart and lean not on your own understanding." Proverbs 3:5

DEVOTIONAL

When we face new and uncertain situations, it can be hard to know what to do. Proverbs 3:5 reminds us to trust God completely, even when things seem unclear. He sees the bigger picture we cannot. Just like a child trusts a loving parent, we can trust that God is guiding us. Whenever you're unsure, take a moment to pray and listen for His guidance. Remember, obedience in the unknown brings us closer to Him and helps us grow in faith.

DAILY REFLECTION

Reflect on a time when you faced a new or uncertain situation. How did you feel, and what did you do to find guidance? In what ways can you remind yourself to trust in God's plan during those moments of uncertainty?

PRAYER

Dear God, when I feel unsure or scared, help me to trust in Your loving plan, knowing that You see everything in a way I cannot. Thank You for guiding me gently, even in moments of uncertainty, so I can grow closer to You.

HE REDEEMS EVERY CHAPTER

"He will redeem Israel from all their iniquities." Psalm 130:8

DEVOTIONAL

God loves each of us perfectly, even when we make mistakes. Psalm 130:8 reminds us that He will redeem Israel from their struggles, just as He redeems us from our mistakes. Every chapter of our lives can lead us closer to Him, no matter how hard things seem. Trust that God is writing your story, turning every setback into a step forward. Embrace His love and know that He is always with you, guiding you to brighter days.

DAILY REFLECTION

How can you remember and trust that God's love is perfectly with you, even when you face challenges or make mistakes? Think about a recent struggle you had, and consider how that experience might help you grow closer to Him.

PRAYER

Dear God, thank you for loving us perfectly, even when we make mistakes. Help us to trust in your promise to turn our struggles into opportunities to grow closer to you and embrace the beautiful story you are writing in our lives.

YOU ARE FULLY KNOWN AND LOVED

"For you created my inmost being; you knit me together in my mother's womb." Psalm 139:13

DEVOTIONAL

You are special because God made you with love! Psalm 139:13 reminds us that God created every part of you, even before you were born. He knows your heart, your dreams, and your struggles. This means you're never alone; you are fully known and loved just as you are. When you feel unsure or lonely, remember that God is always with you, celebrating the wonderful person you are. Take a moment today to thank Him for His amazing love!

DAILY REFLECTION

Think about a time when you felt really special or loved. How does it make you feel to know that God created you with love and knows you completely? Take a moment to share your feelings or write them down.

PRAYER

Dear God, thank you for creating me with love and for knowing every part of who I am. Help me remember that I am special just the way I am, and that you are always with me, reminding me of your amazing love.

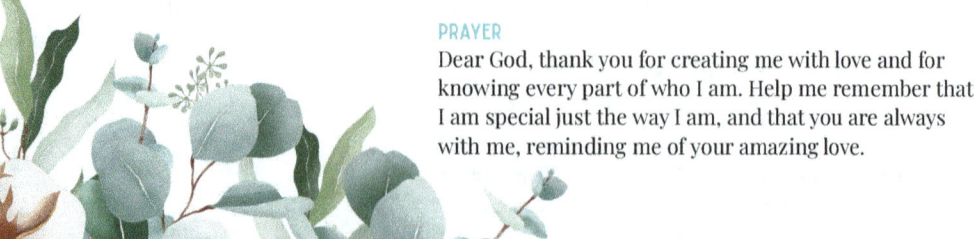

PRAISE AS A WEAPON

"Let everything that has breath praise the Lord." Psalm 150:6

DEVOTIONAL

When we praise God, we release powerful energy that can change our hearts and our day. Psalm 150:6 tells us, "Let everything that has breath praise the Lord." This means you and I, no matter how we feel, can choose to sing, shout, or simply say thank you to God. Praise helps us remember His greatness and goodness. When we lift our voices in joy, we invite God's peace into our lives, making praise a true weapon against worry and fear.

DAILY REFLECTION

Think about a time when you felt worried or fearful. How can you use praise to shift your feelings and invite God's peace into your heart today?

PRAYER

Dear God, thank you for reminding us that when we praise You, we can feel Your peace fill our hearts and chase away our worries. Help us to sing, shout, or simply say thank you, so that we can celebrate Your greatness and invite Your love into our lives today.

UNSHAKEN IN THE STORM

"When you pass through the waters, I will be with you; and through the rivers, they shall not overflow you." Isaiah 43:2

DEVOTIONAL

Life can feel like a storm sometimes, but remember God is always with you. Isaiah 43:2 reminds us that when we face tough times, God promises to be by our side. Imagine walking through a raging river yet feeling safe in His presence. Just as a good friend stands by you, God is even closer during challenging times. When you feel overwhelmed, talk to Him in prayer, and trust that He will keep you unshaken.

DAILY REFLECTION

Reflect on a time when you faced a difficult situation that felt overwhelming. How did you sense God's presence with you during that time? What did you do to talk to Him about your feelings, and how did that help you feel more safe and unshaken?

PRAYER

Dear God, thank You for always being with me, even when life feels like a storm. Help me to remember that just like a good friend, You stand by my side in tough times, and I can share my worries with You to feel safe and unshaken.

CHOOSING TO TRUST AGAIN

"Trust in the Lord with all your heart and lean not on your own understanding."
Proverbs 3:5

DEVOTIONAL

Sometimes, trusting can feel hard, especially when we've been let down. But God reminds us in Proverbs 3:5 to trust Him with all our hearts. This means believing that He cares for us and knows what's best. When we face tough times, instead of relying only on our own thoughts, we can pray and listen to God. Choosing to trust again opens our hearts to His love and guidance. Let's take small steps to believe in Him every day!

DAILY REFLECTION

Reflect on a time when you found it difficult to trust because you felt let down. How can you take a small step today to open your heart to trusting God again? What is one way you can invite Him into your thoughts and feelings during tough times?

PRAYER

Dear God, when trusting feels hard because we've been let down, help us remember that You always care for us and know what's best. Please guide our hearts to take small steps in believing in You, so we can feel Your love and comfort during tough times.

WALKING IN SPIRITUAL WISDOM

"Walk in wisdom toward outsiders, making the best use of the time." Colossians 4:5

DEVOTIONAL

Walking in spiritual wisdom means making thoughtful choices every day. In Colossians 4:5, we learn to show kindness and understanding to everyone we meet. This is especially important with those who may not know God. By being friendly and helpful, we can share a bit of God's love. Remember, every moment is a gift from God! Let's use our time wisely by being good friends, listening well, and showing others how much God cares for them.

DAILY REFLECTION

As you think about your day, consider this: How can you show kindness and understanding to someone you meet today? What are some small, thoughtful choices you can make that reflect God's love?

PRAYER

Dear God, help us to walk in your wisdom today as we make thoughtful choices that show kindness and understanding to everyone we meet. Thank you for each moment you give us to share your love and care with others, guiding us to be good friends and listeners along the way.

THE BLESSING OF SURRENDER

"Trust in the Lord with all your heart and lean not on your own understanding." Proverbs 3:5

DEVOTIONAL

Surrendering to God means trusting Him completely. Proverbs 3:5 reminds us to lean on God, not just our own thoughts. When we let go of our worries and listen for His guidance, we make room for His blessings. It's like sailing a boat; we can't control the wind, but we can adjust our sails to follow it. This week, practice trusting God with your heart. In surrender, you'll find peace and the joy of His presence.

DAILY REFLECTION

How can you take a moment this week to identify a worry or concern in your life and surrender it to God, trusting that He will guide you through it? What changes can you make to adjust your sails and follow His direction instead of relying only on your own understanding?

PRAYER

Dear God, help me to let go of my worries and trust in You completely, knowing that You will guide my heart and mind. As I adjust my sails to follow Your direction, may I feel the peace and joy that comes from surrendering my concerns to Your loving care.

YOUR LIFE IS A LIGHT

"Let your light shine before others, that they may see your good deeds and glorify your Father in heaven." Matthew 5:16

DEVOTIONAL

Your life is like a bright light for others to see! Jesus tells us in Matthew 5:16 to let our light shine. This means doing good things, like being kind and helping others. When we show love and share joy, people notice! They see God's goodness in us and want to know Him too. Remember, even small acts of kindness can brighten someone's day. Shine brightly for Jesus, and let your light lead others to Him.

DAILY REFLECTION

How can you practice kindness today to let your light shine and make someone else's day a little brighter?

PRAYER

Dear Jesus, thank You for reminding us that our lives can shine brightly for others to see Your love. Help us to show kindness and joy today, so that our small acts of goodness may lead others to know You better.

COMFORTED BY GOD'S NEARNESS

"Draw near to God, and He will draw near to you." James 4:8

DEVOTIONAL

When we feel alone or scared, remember that God is always close. James 4:8 tells us that if we want to be near God, we just need to reach out to Him. It's like calling a friend; when you take the first step, they come to you. Spend a few moments talking to God in prayer or reading His Word. You'll find comfort, peace, and a friend who loves you deeply. God is waiting to be near you!

DAILY REFLECTION

When you feel alone or scared, how can you reach out to God and invite Him into your feelings? What are some ways you can remember that He is always close to you?

PRAYER

Dear God, when I feel scared or alone, help me remember that You are always close, just like a good friend. Thank You for being here with me; I invite You into my heart and all my feelings, knowing that Your love brings me comfort and peace.

REFINED THROUGH WAITING

"But those who hope in the Lord will renew their strength. They will soar on wings like eagles; they will run and not grow weary, they will walk and not be faint." Isaiah 40:31

DEVOTIONAL

Waiting can be hard, but it's important in our journey with God. Just like eagles soar high in the sky, we can feel strong and free when we trust in the Lord. When we wait on Him, our strength is renewed, helping us run without getting tired and walk without feeling weak. Remember, God is with us in every moment, preparing us to grow and become even stronger. Let's hope in Him and embrace the waiting!

DAILY REFLECTION

When you think about waiting and trusting in God, what is something you can do to remind yourself that He is with you during that time?

PRAYER

Dear God, thank You for being with us even when we have to wait. Help us to trust in You like the eagles who soar high, knowing that You are renewing our strength and guiding us every step of the way.

GRACE FOR THE PROCESS

"But he said to me, 'My grace is sufficient for you, for my power is made perfect in weakness.'" 2 Corinthians 12:9

DEVOTIONAL

Life can feel overwhelming at times, and we may face challenges that seem too big for us. In these moments, we can remember God's promise: His grace is enough for us! Just like a plant needs time to grow, we need grace as we walk through our struggles. God's strength shines brightest when we feel weak. Trust Him, knowing that He is with you in every step of your journey, helping you become stronger and closer to Him.

DAILY REFLECTION

Think of a time when you felt overwhelmed or faced a challenge that seemed too big. How can you remind yourself that God's grace is enough for you during those tough moments? What steps can you take to trust Him more and feel His strength in your struggles?

PRAYER

Dear God, thank You for being with us when life feels heavy and our challenges seem too big to handle. Please help us to remember Your promise that Your grace is enough, and give us the strength to trust in You more each day, knowing You are always by our side.

CELEBRATING GOD'S FAITHFULNESS

"Great is Your faithfulness." Lamentations 3:23

DEVOTIONAL

Today, let's celebrate God's faithfulness! The Bible tells us, "Great is Your faithfulness" (Lamentations 3:23). This means God always keeps His promises and is with us no matter what. When we feel lonely or scared, we can remember that God is our friend who cares for us. Take a moment to think about the good things God has done in your life. Let gratitude fill your heart, as we trust in His never-ending love and support.

DAILY REFLECTION

What is one good thing that God has done for you that makes you feel grateful, and how can you remember that He is always with you, especially when you feel lonely or scared?

PRAYER

Dear God, thank you for always being with us and for keeping your promises, just like the Bible says. Help us to remember all the good things you have done in our lives, especially when we feel lonely or scared, so that our hearts can be filled with gratitude for your never-ending love.

A Moment of Gratitude

If this devotional has brought moments of peace, strength, or reflection into your life, a short review on Amazon can help others discover it too.

devo.anchoredgraces.com/workingmoms

Even a few words about your experience can make a meaningful difference.

Thank you for continuing this journey.

FINDING PEACE IN THE UNKNOWN

"Be still, and know that I am God." Psalm 46:10

DEVOTIONAL

Sometimes, the future feels uncertain, and that can make us anxious. But remember Psalm 46:10, where God tells us, "Be still, and know that I am God." When life feels confusing, take a moment to breathe and be quiet. In the stillness, you can feel God's presence and peace. Trust that He knows what tomorrow holds. As you seek Him, you will find comfort, knowing He is in control and is always with you.

DAILY REFLECTION

When you think about times when the future feels uncertain, how can you find moments of stillness to connect with God and feel His peace?

PRAYER

Dear God, in moments when the future feels uncertain and my heart feels uneasy, help me to breathe deeply and find stillness, knowing You are here with me. Thank You for Your peace that calms my worries and reminds me that I can trust You with all my tomorrows.

YOU ARE CHOSEN

"But you are a chosen people, a royal priesthood, a holy nation, God's special possession..." 1 Peter 2:9

DEVOTIONAL

You are chosen! Just like a favorite toy, you hold a special place in God's heart. 1 Peter 2:9 tells us that we are a royal family, and God treasures us. Imagine being picked for a wonderful team! God wants you to know that you belong to Him. Each day, remember that you have a unique purpose. Let this truth guide your actions, help you love others, and deepen your friendship with God. You are special!

DAILY REFLECTION

How can you show others that they are special and chosen, just like you are?

PRAYER

Dear God, thank you for choosing me and reminding me that I am special in your eyes. Help me to share your love with others so they can feel how treasured they are, just like I do. Amen.

WHEN YOU NEED DIRECTION

"Trust in the Lord with all your heart and lean not on your own understanding; in all your ways acknowledge Him, and He will direct your paths." Proverbs 3:5-6

DEVOTIONAL

Sometimes, we feel lost and unsure about what to do next. When this happens, remember Proverbs 3:5-6. God invites us to trust Him completely, even when things seem confusing. Instead of relying only on our own thoughts, we can pray and ask Him for help. When we acknowledge Him in our choices, He promises to guide us on the right path. Take a moment each day to seek His direction and feel His loving presence lead you.

DAILY REFLECTION

When you find yourself feeling lost or unsure about what to do next, how can you take a moment to pray and ask God for guidance? What are some specific choices or areas in your life where you can invite Him to help you?

PRAYER

Dear God, when we feel lost or unsure, help us to trust in You and seek Your guidance. Please show us the right path in our choices, so we can feel Your love and presence leading us each day.

ABIDING THROUGH THE CHAOS

"Peace I leave with you; my peace I give you." John 14:27

DEVOTIONAL

In life, we often face chaos and confusion. But Jesus offers us something special—His peace. In John 14:27, He says, "Peace I leave with you; my peace I give you." This peace isn't just the absence of trouble; it's a calm heart that trusts God, even when things seem wild around us. When you feel overwhelmed, take a moment to sit quietly, breathe, and remember that God is with you. Let His peace fill your heart today.

DAILY REFLECTION

When you feel overwhelmed and the world around you feels chaotic, what is one thing you can do to invite God's peace into your heart?

PRAYER

Dear Jesus, when my heart feels heavy and the world seems all mixed up, help me to remember that Your peace is always with me. Teach me to take a quiet moment to breathe and feel Your calmness fill my heart, no matter what is happening around me.

THE STRENGTH TO SAY YES

"I can do all things through Christ who strengthens me." Philippians 4:13

DEVOTIONAL

When we face hard choices, we might feel scared or unsure. But remember, you have the strength of Jesus inside you! Philippians 4:13 tells us, "I can do all things through Christ who strengthens me." This means that whenever you say "yes" to new challenges, whether it's helping a friend or trying something new, Jesus is there to help you. Trust in His strength, and know that you can face anything with Him by your side.

DAILY REFLECTION

Think about a time when you had to make a hard choice. What new challenge did you face, and how can you invite Jesus to help you through that situation? How would you feel knowing He is with you every step of the way?

PRAYER

Dear Jesus, thank you for being with me when I face hard choices and new challenges. Help me to feel your strength inside me, guiding me to trust in you and face everything with courage and love.

GOD'S LOVE NEVER CHANGES

"For I am convinced that neither death nor life, neither angels nor demons, neither the present nor the future, nor any powers, will be able to separate us from the love of God that is in Christ Jesus our Lord." Romans 8:38-39

DEVOTIONAL

God's love is like a strong, unbreakable chain. No matter what happens—whether good or bad—nothing can make God love you less. Romans 8:38-39 reminds us that even the biggest challenges, like death or scary changes, can't pull us away from His love. When you feel alone or worried, remember that God's love is always with you, steady and strong. Take a moment to talk to Him; He's listening and always cares for you, no matter what.

DAILY REFLECTION

Think about a time when you felt alone or scared. How did you remember that God's love was with you, like a strong chain? Take a moment to talk to God about those feelings, and ask Him to help you feel His love even more in those moments. What words do you want to share with Him?

PRAYER

Dear God, thank You for loving me with a love that is strong and unbreakable, just like a chain that holds me close no matter what happens. Help me to feel Your steady presence in moments when I feel scared or alone, and remind me that Your love will always be with me.

HE SEES THE WHOLE PICTURE

"For my thoughts are not your thoughts, neither are your ways my ways, declares the Lord." Isaiah 55:8

DEVOTIONAL

Sometimes, it can feel like everything is confusing or doesn't make sense. But Isaiah 55:8 reminds us that God sees the whole picture, even when we can't. Just like a puzzle, each piece has its place, and God knows how they all fit together. When we trust Him, we can find peace in our hearts. So, whenever you feel lost, remember that God has a greater plan for you, and He loves you deeply. Keep believing!

DAILY REFLECTION

What is one situation in your life right now that feels confusing or unclear, and how can you remind yourself of God's bigger plan and love for you in that moment?

PRAYER

Dear God, when life feels confusing and nothing seems to make sense, help me remember that You see the whole picture and love me deeply. Please fill my heart with peace and remind me to trust in Your greater plan, knowing that everything will fall into place in Your perfect time.

A HEART ALIGNED WITH HIS

"Delight yourself in the Lord, and He will give you the desires of your heart." Psalm 37:4

DEVOTIONAL

When we delight in the Lord, it means we find joy in knowing Him and doing things His way. Think of it like hanging out with a best friend; the more time you spend with God through prayer and reading the Bible, the more your heart starts to match His. As you grow closer to Him, your desires will change, and you'll find that He gives you what truly makes you happy. Keep seeking Him, and trust His plans!

DAILY REFLECTION

As you think about how spending time with God brings you joy, what is one way you can build that friendship with Him this week? Consider how you might pray, read the Bible, or engage in a simple act of kindness that reflects His love.

PRAYER

Dear Lord, thank you for being our best friend and for filling our hearts with joy when we spend time with You. Help us to seek You through prayer and kindness, so our hearts can grow closer to You and reflect Your love in our world.

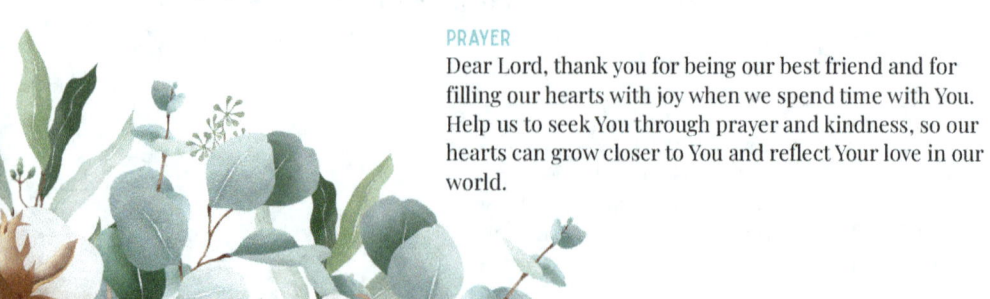

LIVING WITH SPIRITUAL COURAGE

"Be strong and courageous; do not be frightened, and do not be dismayed, for the Lord your God is with you wherever you go." Joshua 1:9

DEVOTIONAL

When we face challenges, it's easy to feel scared or unsure. But God tells us to be strong and courageous because He is always with us! Just like Joshua, we can trust that no matter where we go or what happens, God's presence surrounds us. When you feel afraid, remember to pray and ask for His help. Each day, step forward in faith, knowing that God will guide you through every difficulty. You're never alone!

DAILY REFLECTION

Think about a time when you faced a challenge or felt scared. How did you experience God's presence during that time? What steps can you take today to trust Him more when you feel uncertain?

PRAYER

Dear God, thank you for always being with us, especially when we feel scared or unsure. Help us remember to be strong and courageous, trusting that your love guides us through every challenge we face.

THE PROMISE OF RENEWAL

"Therefore, if anyone is in Christ, he is a new creation; the old has passed away, behold, the new has come." 2 Corinthians 5:17

DEVOTIONAL

God loves us so much! When we believe in Jesus, He makes us new inside. Just like a caterpillar turns into a beautiful butterfly, we can leave behind our old ways. In 2 Corinthians 5:17, we learn that being with Christ means we can start fresh every day. When you wake up, thank God for the new day and ask Him to help you grow. Trust in Him, and you will discover wonderful changes in your life!

DAILY REFLECTION

What are three things you can thank God for today that remind you of the new beginnings He gives you?

PRAYER

Dear God, thank You for loving us so much and for making us new inside through Jesus. Help us to grow and embrace each day as a beautiful new beginning filled with Your wonderful plans for our lives. Today, I can thank You for the beauty of nature, the love of my family, and the joy of friendship that remind me of the fresh starts You give us every day.

CLOTHED IN DIGNITY AND STRENGTH

"She is clothed with strength and dignity; she can laugh at the days to come."
Proverbs 31:25

DEVOTIONAL

In Proverbs 31:25, we learn that a woman of strength and dignity is someone who trusts God. When we wear these qualities like a beautiful garment, we can face each day with joy, no matter what challenges come our way. God gives us courage to laugh at the future because He holds it in His hands. Let us seek strength in His promises and remember that with God, we can embrace each day with confidence and joy.

DAILY REFLECTION

How can you remind yourself of God's promises when facing challenges, and what are some ways you can wear strength and dignity each day, no matter what comes your way?

PRAYER

Dear God, thank you for teaching us that strength and dignity come from trusting in You. Help us to remember Your promises and wear these beautiful qualities each day, so we can face challenges with joy and courage, knowing You hold our future in Your hands.

RUNNING THE RACE WELL

"Let us run with perseverance the race marked out for us, fixing our eyes on Jesus."
Hebrews 12:1-2

DEVOTIONAL

Life is like a race where we all have our unique paths. Hebrews 12:1-2 reminds us to run with perseverance, staying focused on Jesus, who guides us. Just like a runner keeps their eyes on the finish line, we should keep our hearts set on Him. When challenges arise, remember that Jesus is with you, helping you take each step with strength. Trust Him, stay committed, and you'll find joy in every stride of your journey.

DAILY REFLECTION

As you think about your unique journey, how can you stay focused on Jesus when facing challenges, and what steps can you take to embrace the joy in each part of your race?

PRAYER

Dear God, thank you for guiding us on our unique paths like a loving coach who encourages us to keep running with joy, even when the race gets tough. Help us to stay focused on Jesus, trusting Him to give us strength and reminding us that each step we take is part of our beautiful journey with You.

STILLNESS IN GOD'S PRESENCE

"Be still, and know that I am God." Psalm 46:10

DEVOTIONAL

In our busy days, it's easy to forget to pause. Psalm 46:10 tells us, "Be still, and know that I am God." This means taking a moment to breathe and feel God's love. When we sit quietly, we can hear His gentle voice guiding us. Spend a few minutes each day in stillness, maybe during breakfast or before bedtime. As you do, God will fill your heart with peace and wisdom, helping you grow closer to Him.

DAILY REFLECTION

When you take a moment to be still today, what are some thoughts or feelings that come to you about God's goodness? How can you use this time to listen for His guidance?

PRAYER

Dear God, thank you for reminding us to be still and feel your loving presence in our busy lives. Help us to pause and listen for your gentle guidance, filling our hearts with peace and joy as we grow closer to you.

YOUR FAITH CAN MOVE MOUNTAINS

"For truly, I say to you, if you have faith like a grain of mustard seed, you will say to this mountain, 'Move from here to there,' and it will move, and nothing will be impossible for you."
Matthew 17:20

DEVOTIONAL

Have you ever seen a tiny mustard seed? It's small, but it can grow into a huge plant! Jesus tells us that even a little faith, like that tiny seed, can do amazing things. When we trust God, we can face our biggest challenges. Imagine telling a mountain to move—Jesus says it's possible with faith! So, when you feel scared or stuck, remember to believe. God is with you, and your faith can help you overcome anything.

DAILY REFLECTION

Think about a time when you faced something that felt really big or scary. What helped you to feel brave and trust that you could handle it? How can you remember to use your faith like a tiny mustard seed when challenges come your way?

PRAYER

Dear God, thank you for the tiny mustard seed that reminds us that even small faith can grow into something wonderful. Help us to trust in you when we face challenges, knowing that with our belief, we can find strength and courage to overcome anything.

LET GOD REWRITE YOUR STORY

"Therefore, if anyone is in Christ, he is a new creation; the old has passed away, behold, the new has come." 2 Corinthians 5:17

DEVOTIONAL

Sometimes we might feel like our past mistakes define us. But 2 Corinthians 5:17 reminds us that in Christ, we are made new! Just like an artist painting over an old canvas, God takes our messy lives and rewrites our stories with love and grace. Each day, we can ask Him to help us grow and walk in our new identity. Trust that God has amazing plans for you, and let Him create a beautiful story in your life!

DAILY REFLECTION

How can you remind yourself of your new identity in Christ when you start to feel weighed down by your past mistakes? Consider the ways God has already transformed your life and how you can invite Him to continue painting a beautiful story for you each day.

PRAYER

Dear God, thank You for making us new and reminding us that our past mistakes do not define who we are. Help us remember Your love and grace as we grow each day, inviting You to paint a beautiful story in our lives.

COMPASSION IN ACTION

"Be kind and compassionate to one another, forgiving each other, just as in Christ God forgave you." Ephesians 4:32

DEVOTIONAL

Compassion in action means showing kindness to those around us, just like Jesus did. Ephesians 4:32 reminds us to forgive others, just as God forgives us. When we treat people with love and kindness, we reflect God's heart. Think about a time you felt sad or hurt; remember how good it felt when someone showed you kindness. Today, look for opportunities to be a friend, help someone, or simply listen. Let your heart be a light in someone else's life!

DAILY REFLECTION

Think about a time when someone showed you kindness when you were feeling sad or hurt. How did that make you feel? Today, can you think of a way you can show kindness to someone else who might need a friend or a listening ear? What small act of compassion can you choose to do?

PRAYER

Dear God, help us to open our hearts and share kindness with those around us, just like Jesus showed us. May we always look for ways to lend a hand or listen to someone who needs a friend, reflecting Your love in all we do.

THE POWER OF A QUIET YES

"Let your 'yes' be yes, and your 'no,' no." Matthew 5:37

DEVOTIONAL

In our busy lives, it can be easy to say "yes" without thinking. But God teaches us to be honest and thoughtful. When we say "yes," let it come from our hearts. A quiet "yes" means we are sure and ready to help. It reflects trust in God's plan. Today, consider the power of your words. Are your "yes" and "no" true? Ask God to guide you. When we choose wisely, we grow closer to Him and strengthen our faith.

DAILY REFLECTION

Think about a time when you said "yes" to something. How did it make you feel, and do you think it came from your heart? Take a moment to ask God for guidance on how to choose your words wisely and to ensure that your "yes" and "no" are true reflections of your intentions. What can you do to make sure your responses align with your trust in God's plan?

PRAYER

Dear God, please help me to think carefully before I say "yes" or "no," so my words truly reflect what's in my heart. Guide me to choose wisely, trusting in Your plan, and to always share love and kindness with others through my responses.

CELEBRATING GOD'S GOODNESS

"Give thanks to the Lord, for he is good; his love endures forever." Psalm 107:1

DEVOTIONAL

Today, let's remember to celebrate God's goodness! Psalm 107:1 tells us to give thanks because God is good and His love lasts forever. Take a moment to look around you. Notice the sunshine, the laughter of friends, or even a delicious meal. These are gifts from God, showing His love for us. When we say "thank you," we open our hearts to feel His joy. Let's practice gratitude every day and grow closer to Him!

DAILY REFLECTION

What are three things you see or hear right now that remind you of God's goodness? How can you share your gratitude for those gifts with others today?

PRAYER

Dear God, thank you for all the wonderful things around us that show your goodness and love, like the warm sunshine and laughter of friends. Help us to notice the gifts you give each day and share our gratitude with those around us, spreading your joy and kindness.

YOUR VOICE MATTERS

"Let everything that has breath praise the Lord." Psalm 150:6

DEVOTIONAL

Your voice matters! Psalm 150:6 reminds us that everyone and everything that breathes should praise the Lord. Every time you sing, pray, or even speak kind words, you're sharing your unique sound that God loves to hear. Your voice is special, just like you! Use it to express joy, gratitude, or encouragement to others. Remember, God loves when you talk to Him or share your heart. Keep using your voice to bring light and love into the world!

DAILY REFLECTION

How can you use your voice today to express joy, gratitude, or encouragement to someone around you? Think of a specific way you can share your unique sound and make a positive impact in their life.

PRAYER

Dear God, thank You for giving me a voice that can share joy and love with others. Help me to use my words today to lift someone up and remind them how special they are, just like You created each of us to be.

HE DELIGHTS IN YOU

"The Lord your God is in your midst, a mighty one who will save; he will rejoice over you with gladness; he will quiet you by his love; he will exult over you with loud singing." Zephaniah 3:17

DEVOTIONAL

God is always close to you, and He loves you deeply. In Zephaniah 3:17, we learn that He is mighty and ready to help you when you need it. Imagine God rejoicing over you with great joy, like a loving parent celebrating a child's successes. When you feel scared or alone, remember that His love can bring you peace. Trust in His joy for you, and know that you are wonderfully made and cherished. Let His love fill your heart today!

DAILY REFLECTION

How does it make you feel to think about God rejoicing over you, and in what ways can you remember His love when you face fears or feelings of being alone?

PRAYER

Dear God, thank you for being so close to me and loving me deeply; I am grateful that You rejoice over me with joy. Help me remember Your love when I feel scared or alone, and fill my heart with peace as I trust in Your mighty presence.

PURSUING GOD OVER PERFECTION

"But seek first the kingdom of God and His righteousness, and all these things will be added to you." Matthew 6:33

DEVOTIONAL

Sometimes we think we must be perfect to please God, but that's not true! In Matthew 6:33, Jesus tells us to seek God and His goodness first. This means when we focus on loving Him and following His ways, everything else will fall into place. Remember, it's okay to make mistakes; God loves us no matter what. Each day, let's choose to spend time with Him and trust that He will help us grow in His love.

DAILY REFLECTION

Reflect on a time when you felt pressured to be perfect or do everything right. How did that make you feel? What would it look like for you to focus more on seeking God's love and trusting Him, rather than trying to be perfect?

PRAYER

Dear God, thank you for loving us just as we are and reminding us that we don't have to be perfect to be close to you. Help us to seek your goodness and trust in your love, knowing that each day is a new chance to grow in your grace.

BRAVE STEPS OF OBEDIENCE

"For we walk by faith, not by sight." 2 Corinthians 5:7

DEVOTIONAL

Walking by faith means trusting God even when we can't see the way ahead. Just like taking a brave step into a dark room, we might feel scared at first, but God promises to be our light. When we obey Him, we discover new paths and grow stronger in our faith. Remember, every small step of obedience brings us closer to God. Let's walk together, trusting Him to lead us where He wants us to go.

DAILY REFLECTION

What is one way you can take a brave step of faith today, even if you can't see what lies ahead, and how can you trust God to guide you in that step?

PRAYER

Dear God, help us to trust you like a child stepping into the unknown, knowing that you will be our guiding light even when we can't see the path ahead. Teach us to take brave steps of faith, believing in your love and guidance, as we grow closer to you each day.

FAITH THAT OVERFLOWS

"And hope does not put us to shame, because God's love has been poured out into our hearts through the Holy Spirit, who has been given to us." Romans 5:5

DEVOTIONAL

Faith is like a fountain that overflows! When we trust in God, His love fills our hearts and spills out to everyone around us. Just like a warm hug, God's love brings us hope and joy, reminding us that we are never alone. Each day, let's invite the Holy Spirit to fill us up so we can share His love with family and friends. Remember, when we have faith, our hearts can glow with God's light!

DAILY REFLECTION

How can you let God's love overflow from your heart into the lives of those around you today? Think of one way you can share His joy and hope with your family or friends.

PRAYER

Dear God, thank you for filling our hearts with Your love like a fountain that overflows. Help us share Your joy and hope with everyone around us, so they can feel Your warmth and never know loneliness.

FINDING COMFORT IN SCRIPTURE

"All Scripture is God-breathed and is useful for teaching, rebuking, correcting and training in righteousness." 2 Timothy 3:16

DEVOTIONAL

When we read the Bible, we remember it comes from God. Just like a cozy blanket on a chilly day, Scripture brings comfort to our hearts. It teaches us how to live well, encourages us when we're down, corrects us when we stray, and helps us grow closer to God. Each verse is like a loving hug, reminding us that we're never alone. Let's take time each day to explore these words and feel His warmth surround us.

DAILY REFLECTION

How can you find comfort in a Bible verse this week, and what is one way you can share that comfort with someone else who might need it?

PRAYER

Dear God, thank you for giving us the Bible, which wraps our hearts in love and comfort like a cozy blanket. Help us to find joy in Your words this week and to share that warmth with someone who needs it.

STRENGTH FOR THE SURRENDER

"My grace is sufficient for you, for my power is made perfect in weakness." 2 Corinthians 12:9

DEVOTIONAL

When we feel weak or anxious, it can be hard to trust God. But in 2 Corinthians 12:9, God reminds us that His grace is enough. Imagine climbing a big mountain and feeling tired. Instead of giving up, we can pause and ask for help. God's strength shines brightest when we feel weak. Surrendering our worries to Him brings peace. This week, remember: when you feel weak, God's grace will lift you, making you strong in His love.

DAILY REFLECTION

When you feel weak or anxious this week, what is one way you can remind yourself to ask God for help and trust in His grace?

PRAYER

Dear God, when we feel weak or anxious, help us to remember that Your grace is always with us, inviting us to ask for Your strength. May we trust in Your love and find peace, knowing that You are right beside us during our struggles.

YOU WERE MADE FOR THIS SEASON

"For I know the plans I have for you, declares the Lord, plans to prosper you and not to harm you, plans to give you hope and a future." Jeremiah 29:11

DEVOTIONAL

In every season of life, remember that you were made for this time. Just like God promised in Jeremiah 29:11, He has special plans for you—plans filled with hope and a bright future. Even when things are tough, trust that God is working in you and through you. Take a moment each day to pray, listen, and believe that you are exactly where you need to be. Embrace this season, knowing that God's love surrounds you always.

DAILY REFLECTION

How can you embrace your current season of life and recognize the ways God is working in you? Take a moment to think about what you can do each day to trust in His plans for you.

PRAYER

Dear God, thank You for reminding me that I am here for a special purpose and that Your love surrounds me every day. Help me to see the good in my current season of life and to trust in the wonderful plans You have for me, knowing that You are always working in my heart.

THE ANCHOR OF GOD'S WORD

"Your word is a lamp to my feet and a light to my path."
Psalm 119:105

DEVOTIONAL

God's Word is like a bright lamp that helps us see our way, even when the path feels dark or uncertain. Just as we need light to walk safely, we need the Bible to guide our hearts and minds. When we read and remember God's promises, we can trust that He is with us, showing us the best way to go. Let's treasure His words and let them light our paths every day!

DAILY REFLECTION

How has reading or remembering a promise from God helped you feel more secure or confident during a difficult time?

PRAYER

Dear God, thank you for your wonderful Word that shines like a bright light, helping us find our way even when things feel a bit scary or unsure. Please help us to treasure your promises in our hearts, knowing that you are always with us, guiding us to make good choices each day.

TRUSTING HIM, EVEN IN SILENCE

"Blessed is the one who trusts in the Lord, whose confidence is in him." Jeremiah 17:7

DEVOTIONAL

Sometimes, it feels quiet, and we wonder if God hears us. But remember, trusting Him means believing He is always with us, even in silence. Just like a tree grows strong with roots deep in the soil, we can grow in faith by resting in His love. Jeremiah 17:7 reminds us that we are blessed when we trust in the Lord. Let's choose to believe that He is working for our good, even when we can't see it.

DAILY REFLECTION

How can you remind yourself to trust in God's presence during moments when you feel quiet or unsure? What are some ways you can feel connected to Him even when you can't see what He is doing in your life?

PRAYER

Dear God, even in the quiet moments when we feel unsure, help us to trust that You are always with us and working for our good. May we find comfort in Your love, just like a tree grows strong with deep roots, and remember to look for Your presence in our hearts and the world around us.

LIVING GRATEFULLY

"Give thanks in all circumstances; for this is the will of God in Christ Jesus for you."
1 Thessalonians 5:18

DEVOTIONAL

Gratitude is a powerful way to connect with God. In 1 Thessalonians 5:18, we learn to "give thanks in all circumstances." This means we can thank God not just for the good days, but even during tough times. When we focus on what we are grateful for, we see God's love more clearly. Try making a list of things you are thankful for each day. It's a wonderful way to grow closer to God and celebrate His blessings in your life.

DAILY REFLECTION

Reflect on a recent challenging experience in your life. What are three things you can find to be grateful for in that situation? How do these gratitude points help you see God's love and presence during tough times?

PRAYER

Dear God, thank you for each blessing in my life, even the ones that feel tough, for they help me see Your love in new ways. Please remind me to always find something to be grateful for, so that I can grow closer to You and feel Your gentle presence guiding me.

YOUR STORY REFLECTS HIS GLORY

"Let your light shine before others, that they may see your good deeds and glorify your Father in heaven." Matthew 5:16

DEVOTIONAL

Your story is part of a bigger story—God's story. Each time you do something kind or helpful, you shine your light and show others how great God is. Remember, everything you do can help others see how amazing He is. When you share love, joy, and kindness, you make God's glory visible to the world. Let your actions reflect His goodness today, and know that you are shining a light that leads others to Him.

DAILY REFLECTION

Think about a time when you did something kind for someone else. How did that make you feel, and in what ways do you think your actions helped others see God's goodness?

PRAYER

Dear God, thank you for letting me be a part of your wonderful story. Help me to show kindness and love today, so others can see how amazing you are through my actions.

WALKING IN THE LIGHT

"But if we walk in the light, as he is in the light, we have fellowship with one another."
1 John 1:7

DEVOTIONAL

Walking in the light means living in God's truth and love. When we choose to follow Jesus, we shine His light in our lives. This light helps us see what is right and good, and it brings us closer to God and to our friends. Each day, let's choose kindness, honesty, and love, showing God's light to everyone around us. Remember, when we walk in the light together, we grow stronger in our faith and friendships.

DAILY REFLECTION

Reflect on a moment this week when you felt the light of God's truth and love in your life. How did that experience help you see what is right and good? In what ways can you choose to share that light with someone else today?

PRAYER

Dear God, thank you for your light that fills our hearts with love and truth, guiding us to be kind and honest with ourselves and others. Help us to share this precious light with everyone we meet, so together, we can grow stronger in faith and friendship.

GRATITUDE IN EVERY CIRCUMSTANCE

"Give thanks in all circumstances; for this is the will of God in Christ Jesus for you." 1 Thessalonians 5:18

DEVOTIONAL

Life can be full of ups and downs, but 1 Thessalonians 5:18 reminds us to give thanks in every situation. When things go well, it's easy to be grateful, but even when we face challenges, there's always something to appreciate. Maybe it's a lesson learned or the love of friends and family. Practicing gratitude helps us grow closer to God. This week, take a moment each day to find something to be thankful for, and watch your heart fill with joy.

DAILY REFLECTION

As you think about your week, what is one challenge you faced that helped you discover something to be thankful for? How did that experience bring you closer to God?

PRAYER

Dear God, thank you for reminding us to find goodness even in tough times, and for the love and lessons that help us grow. May we always open our hearts to gratitude, so we can feel your presence and joy in every moment of our lives.

HE IS FAITHFUL STILL

"Let us hold unswervingly to the hope we profess, for he who promised is faithful." Hebrews 10:23

DEVOTIONAL

God is faithful, even when times are tough. In Hebrews 10:23, we're reminded to hold onto our hope because God always keeps His promises. Just like a good friend who never lets you down, God is always there for you. When you feel alone or unsure, remember that His love is unchanging. Take a moment to pray and trust Him with your worries. By doing this, you're growing closer to Him and discovering His faithfulness in your life.

DAILY REFLECTION

Think about a time when you felt worried or uncertain. How can remembering God's faithfulness and promises help you find peace in those moments? What specific worries can you lift up to Him in prayer today?

PRAYER

Dear God, thank you for always being there for me, just like a trusted friend who never lets me down. When I feel worried or unsure, help me to remember your promises and your unchanging love, so I can find peace in my heart.

STRENGTH IN SURRENDER

"Come to me, all you who are weary and burdened, and I will give you rest." Matthew 11:28

DEVOTIONAL

When we feel tired, worried, or heavy-hearted, God invites us to come to Him. In Matthew 11:28, He promises rest for our weary souls. This means we can share our worries with Him and let go of what burdens us. Surrendering our worries can be hard, but it brings us closer to God. Trust that He cares for you and wants to help. When you release your burdens, you'll find peace and strength in His loving arms.

DAILY REFLECTION

When you feel tired or overwhelmed, what are some specific worries or burdens you can share with God, and how might releasing those worries help you feel closer to Him?

PRAYER

Dear God, when I feel tired or worried, I come to You with an open heart, sharing my burdens and fears. Help me to let go of what weighs me down, so I can feel Your loving arms around me and find peace in Your care.

THE POWER OF REMEMBERING

"Remember the wonders he has done, his miracles, and the judgments he pronounced." Psalm 105:5

DEVOTIONAL

Remembering God's wonders helps us see His greatness in our lives. Psalm 105:5 reminds us to think about all the amazing things He has done. When we remember His miracles, we grow closer to Him and strengthen our faith. Take a moment each day to recall a special blessing or a time God helped you. This practice not only fills our hearts with gratitude but also encourages us to trust Him even more in the future.

DAILY REFLECTION

What is one special moment when you felt God's presence in your life, and how does remembering that moment help you trust Him more today?

PRAYER

Dear God, thank you for all the wonderful things you have done in our lives; help us to remember your miracles and blessings each day. As we think about the special moments where we felt your presence, may our hearts fill with gratitude and our trust in you grow ever stronger.

WALKING THROUGH GRIEF WITH GOD

"Blessed are those who mourn, for they will be comforted." Matthew 5:4

DEVOTIONAL

When we feel sad and miss someone we love, it's okay to cry and be sad. Jesus tells us in Matthew 5:4 that those who mourn are blessed because they will be comforted. Imagine God wrapping His arms around you, helping to heal your heart. You can talk to Him about your feelings, and He will listen. Remember, it's in our sorrow that we can feel God's love the most. Trust Him to walk with you through your grief.

DAILY REFLECTION

When you feel sad and miss someone you love, how can you talk to God about your feelings and imagine Him comforting you in those moments?

PRAYER

Dear God, when I feel sad and miss someone I love, help me to remember that it's okay to cry and share my feelings with You. Please wrap Your loving arms around my heart and bring me comfort as I trust in Your presence during these hard times.

REST FOR THE WEARY

"Come to me, all you who are weary and burdened, and I will give you rest." Matthew 11:28

DEVOTIONAL

Feeling tired and overwhelmed is part of life, but Jesus invites us to find rest in Him. In Matthew 11:28, He says, "Come to me, all you who are weary and burdened, and I will give you rest." When you feel heavy with worries or fears, remember that you can talk to Jesus. He understands your struggles and offers peace. Take a moment to pray, close your eyes, and let His love refresh your spirit today.

DAILY REFLECTION

Reflect on a time when you felt tired or overwhelmed. How did you respond to those feelings? Now, think about how you can invite Jesus into those moments of weariness. What specific worries or fears can you bring to Him today, and how do you hope to feel after sharing those with Him?

PRAYER

Dear Jesus, when I feel tired and overwhelmed, I remember Your invitation to come to You for rest; please help me to lay down my worries and fears at Your feet and find peace in Your love. Comfort my heart and refresh my spirit, knowing that You understand my struggles and are always here to support me.

FINDING CONTENTMENT IN CHRIST

"I have learned to be content whatever the circumstances." Philippians 4:11

DEVOTIONAL

In Philippians 4:11, Paul teaches us about contentment. He says he has learned to be happy no matter what is happening around him. We can find joy in all circumstances by trusting in Jesus. When we focus on Him, we realize that true happiness doesn't come from what we have, but from knowing God loves us. Today, take a moment to thank God for what you have and remember that Jesus is your greatest treasure.

DAILY REFLECTION

Reflect on a time when you felt content or happy, even when things weren't perfect. What helped you find joy in that moment? How can you remind yourself to focus on Jesus as your greatest treasure when you're facing challenges?

PRAYER

Dear God, thank you for always being with us and reminding us that true happiness comes from knowing your love, not from what we own. Help us to treasure Jesus in our hearts and to find joy in every moment, even when things aren't perfect.

YOU ARE HELD

"For I hold you by your right hand—I, the Lord your God. And I say to you, 'Don't be afraid. I am here to help you.'" Isaiah 41:13

DEVOTIONAL

Even when you feel scared or alone, remember that God is right beside you, holding your hand. Just like a parent or friend offers comfort, God promises to help you. When you face challenges, think of Isaiah 41:13. God says, "Don't be afraid. I am here to help you." Trust in His love and strength. Each day, take a moment to feel His presence and let Him guide you. You are never alone; you are always held in His care.

DAILY REFLECTION

When you feel scared or alone, who can you reach out to for comfort, and how can you remind yourself that God is with you during tough times?

PRAYER

Dear God, thank you for being with me and holding my hand when I feel scared or alone. Help me remember that I can always reach out to you and those I love for comfort, knowing that your love and strength guide me through every challenge.

A SPIRIT OF THANKSGIVING

"Give thanks in all circumstances; for this is the will of God in Christ Jesus for you."
1 Thessalonians 5:18

DEVOTIONAL

Every day brings a chance to say thank you to God! In 1 Thessalonians 5:18, we learn to give thanks in all circumstances. This means even when things are tough, we can find something good. Maybe it's a warm hug, a sunny day, or time with friends and family. When we choose to be grateful, we grow closer to God. Today, take a moment to think about what you're thankful for. Let that joy fill your heart!

DAILY REFLECTION

Think about a time this week when you faced a challenge. What is one positive thing you can find in that situation that you can thank God for? How does recognizing that good thing make you feel?

PRAYER

Dear God, thank you for all the special moments in our lives, even when things are tough. Help us to see the good in every situation and fill our hearts with gratitude, so we can grow closer to you each day.

WHEN GOD FEELS DISTANT

"Draw near to God, and He will draw near to you." James 4:8

DEVOTIONAL

Sometimes, it can feel like God is far away, especially when we face challenges or feel alone. But remember, the Bible tells us in James 4:8, "Draw near to God, and He will draw near to you." This means that when we take steps toward God—like praying, reading the Bible, or being kind to others—He promises to come closer to us. Let's spend time with Him today, knowing that He is always ready to listen and be with us.

DAILY REFLECTION

Think about a time when you felt alone or faced a challenge. What is one way you can reach out to God today—perhaps through prayer, reading a Bible verse, or showing kindness to someone? How do you think that will help you feel closer to Him?

PRAYER

Dear God, sometimes it feels like we are all alone, but I know that when I reach out to You, You come closer to me. Help me to be brave and take steps toward You today, whether through prayer, reading Your words, or being kind to someone in need. Amen.

PEACE THAT PASSES UNDERSTANDING

"And the peace of God, which transcends all understanding, will guard your hearts and your minds in Christ Jesus." Philippians 4:7

DEVOTIONAL

When we face worries or tough times, it's easy to feel alone and afraid. But God promises us a special peace that goes beyond what we can understand. Think of it as a warm blanket that wraps around our hearts and minds, keeping us safe. When we trust in Jesus and pray, this peace helps us stay calm and brave. Remember, even when life gets hard, God is with you, offering comfort and strength every step of the way.

DAILY REFLECTION

What do you think it feels like to have God's peace wrapped around you like a warm blanket during tough times? Can you remember a moment when you felt that comfort, and how did it help you?

PRAYER

Dear God, thank you for your promise of peace that wraps around us like a warm blanket, helping us feel safe and brave even when things get tough. Help us to trust in you, remembering that you are always with us, offering comfort and strength in every moment we face.

HE RESTORES WHAT WAS BROKEN

"He heals the brokenhearted and binds up their wounds." Psalm 147:3

DEVOTIONAL

Sometimes, we feel sad or hurt inside, just like a broken toy that needs fixing. But God loves us so much! Psalm 147:3 tells us that He heals our broken hearts and helps us feel better. When life gets tough, we can talk to God and ask Him to make us whole again. Remember, He's always there to mend our wounds and fill our hearts with joy. Trust in Him, and you will find peace!

DAILY REFLECTION

How can you remember to talk to God when you feel sad or hurt, just like a broken toy needs to be fixed?

PRAYER

Dear God, when we feel sad or broken inside, help us remember that You are always here to heal our hearts and bring us joy. Thank You for loving us so much, and please remind us to talk to You whenever we need comfort and strength.

YOU ARE CALLED AND EQUIPPED

"For we are God's handiwork, created in Christ Jesus to do good works, which God prepared in advance for us to do." Ephesians 2:10

DEVOTIONAL

You are uniquely made by God, just as a beautiful piece of art. In Ephesians 2:10, we learn that God created you to do good things, things that He planned just for you! Each day is an opportunity to discover and fulfill those special tasks. Remember, you are not alone; God equips you with everything you need. Trust Him to guide you in doing good works, sharing love, and making a difference in the world around you.

DAILY REFLECTION

What are some good things you believe God has planned for you to do today, and how can you share love with those around you?

PRAYER

Dear God, thank you for making me unique and giving me special things to do every day. Help me to trust you as I share love and kindness with those around me, and guide me in discovering the good works you have planned for me.

HOPE THAT ANCHORS

"We have this hope as an anchor for the soul, firm and secure." Hebrews 6:19

DEVOTIONAL

Hope is like an anchor that keeps our hearts steady, even when life gets stormy. When you feel scared or uncertain, remember that God is always there to hold you firm. He promises that His love and presence are unchanging. Just as an anchor keeps a ship safe in rough waters, God's hope keeps our souls safe. This week, take a moment to trust in Him. Let His hope guide you, and you will find peace in every situation.

DAILY REFLECTION

Think about a time when you felt scared or uncertain, like being in a storm. How can remembering God's hope help you feel steadier and more secure in those moments? What is one way you can trust in Him this week?

PRAYER

Dear God, thank You for being our anchor of hope when the storms of life make us feel scared or unsure. Please help us to remember Your constant love and be brave in trusting You this week, knowing that You will keep our hearts steady in every wave we face.

A GRATEFUL HEART IS A STRONG HEART

"Give thanks in all circumstances; for this is the will of God in Christ Jesus for you." 1 Thessalonians 5:18

DEVOTIONAL

A grateful heart is like a strong superhero! When we thank God in everything, we open our eyes to the good around us. Even when things feel tough, saying "thank you" helps us remember God's love and care. In 1 Thessalonians 5:18, God reminds us to give thanks in all circumstances. This strengthens our faith, helping us grow closer to Him. Today, let's find something to be thankful for and watch how it makes our hearts strong!

DAILY REFLECTION

What is one thing you can thank God for today, and how does recognizing that help you feel stronger in your faith?

PRAYER

Dear God, thank you for always being with us and for all the blessings we have, even when things feel hard. Help us to see the good around us and remember that by being grateful, our hearts grow strong in your love.

LETTING GO OF WHAT NO LONGER SERVES

"Forget the former things; do not dwell on the past." Isaiah 43:18

DEVOTIONAL

Sometimes, we hold on to old things that keep us from moving forward—bad memories, mistakes, or even worries. In Isaiah 43:18, God reminds us to "forget the former things" and not dwell on the past. This means it's time to let go of what no longer helps us. Instead, focus on the new adventures God has for you! Trust that He is doing something amazing in your life, and embrace all the good things ahead.

DAILY REFLECTION

What is one old memory or worry that you can let go of today, and how can focusing on the new things God has in store for you help you move forward?

PRAYER

Dear God, help me let go of the worries and old memories that hold me back, trusting in the exciting new adventures You have planned for me. Fill my heart with hope as I focus on the good things ahead, knowing that You are always by my side.

FAITH IN THE FIRE

"When you go through deep waters, I will be with you." Isaiah 43:2

DEVOTIONAL

When we face tough times, it's easy to feel alone and scared. But God promises us that He is always by our side, even in the deepest waters. Just like a warm hug during a storm, His love comforts us. Remember, the fire may feel intense, but it helps us grow stronger and more like Him. Trust that God is with you every step of the way, guiding you through challenges and helping you shine brighter than before.

DAILY REFLECTION

Think about a time when you faced a tough situation. How did you feel in that moment, and what helped you remember that God was with you?

PRAYER

Dear God, when I'm feeling scared and alone during tough times, help me remember that Your love surrounds me like a warm hug. Guide me through the challenges, and remind me that I can grow stronger and shine brighter with Your light always by my side.

THE BLESSING OF TODAY

"This is the day that the Lord has made; let us rejoice and be glad in it." Psalm 118:24

DEVOTIONAL

Today is a special gift from God, and it's a chance for us to celebrate! Psalm 118:24 reminds us that every day is made by Him, filled with opportunities to see His love and grace. Look around you today—there's beauty in the simple things: the sun shining, a friend's smile, or a moment of kindness. Let's choose to be happy and thankful, remembering that God is with us in every moment. Let's rejoice in today!

DAILY REFLECTION

What small thing have you noticed today that reminds you of God's love and grace? How can you celebrate that moment and share your happiness with someone else?

PRAYER

Dear God, thank You for the wonderful gift of today, filled with all the little joys that remind us of Your love. Help us to notice the beauty around us and to share that happiness with others, celebrating Your grace in every moment.

PREPARING YOUR HEART FOR WORSHIP

"Draw near to God, and he will draw near to you." James 4:8

DEVOTIONAL

As we prepare for worship, it's important to remember James 4:8: "Draw near to God, and he will draw near to you." Think of worship as a special time with God. To get ready, we can set aside distractions, pray, and open our hearts. When we sincerely seek God, He promises to come closer to us. Each time we worship, we grow in love and understanding. Let's make that space in our hearts for Him today!

DAILY REFLECTION

As you prepare for worship today, what are some distractions you can set aside to create space in your heart for God? How do you feel when you think about drawing near to Him?

PRAYER

Dear God, as we get ready to spend time with You, help us to put away anything that distracts our hearts so we can truly draw near to You. May we feel Your love wrap around us, reminding us how special this time together is.

TRUST THAT TRIUMPHS

"Trust in the Lord with all your heart and lean not on your own understanding."
Proverbs 3:5

DEVOTIONAL

Trusting God means believing He is always with us, even when we feel unsure. When we face challenges or big decisions, Proverbs 3:5 reminds us to trust Him completely, instead of relying on our own thoughts. Just like a child trusts a parent to guide them, we can trust God to lead us in the right direction. Let's choose to believe in His love and wisdom, knowing that He always has our best interests at heart.

DAILY REFLECTION

How can you practice trusting God in your life, especially when you face challenges or big decisions? Take a moment to think about a specific situation where you can lean on His guidance instead of relying solely on your own thoughts.

PRAYER

Dear God, thank you for always being with me, even when things feel uncertain. Help me to trust in your love and wisdom as I face challenges and make decisions, knowing you are guiding me every step of the way.

THANKFULNESS AS WORSHIP

"Enter his gates with thanksgiving and his courts with praise; give thanks to him and praise his name." Psalm 100:4

DEVOTIONAL

Thankfulness is a special way to show God we love Him! Psalm 100:4 tells us to enter His gates with thanksgiving and praise. When we start our day with grateful hearts, we invite God into our lives. Think about your blessings: a warm home, loving family, and friends. Each time you say "thank you," you are worshiping God. Let's make it a habit to express our gratitude daily, growing closer to Him and spreading joy everywhere we go!

DAILY REFLECTION

What are three things you are thankful for today, and how can you share that gratitude with someone else to show your love for God?

PRAYER

Dear God, thank you for the many gifts you give us every day, like our warm home, loving family, and wonderful friends. Help us to share our gratitude with others so they can feel your love through our kind words and actions.

GOD'S GOODNESS NEVER FAILS

"For the Lord is good; his steadfast love endures forever, and his faithfulness to all generations." Psalm 100:5

DEVOTIONAL

God is always good, just like the sun that shines every day! Psalm 100:5 reminds us that His love never fades, no matter what happens. When we face tough times or feel lonely, we can remember that God is our friend, never leaving us alone. His faithfulness lasts forever, helping us grow in our trust and love for Him. Let's talk to God, thank Him for His goodness, and share His love with others every day!

DAILY REFLECTION

How can you share a moment when you felt God's goodness this week, and how can you remind yourself and others about His love during tough times?

PRAYER

Dear God, thank you for being good and shining Your love on us just like the sun every day. Help us to remember You are always with us, especially when we feel lonely or face hard times, and guide us to share Your kindness and love with everyone we meet.

CELEBRATING SMALL THINGS

"Every good and perfect gift is from above." James 1:17

DEVOTIONAL

Every day, God gives us small, special gifts that brighten our lives. Think about the sunshine that warms your face or the laughter of friends. James 1:17 reminds us that every good and perfect gift comes from God. Today, let's take a moment to celebrate these little blessings. Make a list of things that make you smile—like your favorite snack or a pretty flower. Thank God for these gifts, and remember, noticing the little things helps us grow closer to Him.

DAILY REFLECTION

What are three small things you notice around you every day that bring you joy, and how can you show gratitude to God for these gifts?

PRAYER

Dear God, thank you for the little gifts that make our days brighter—like the warmth of the sun on our skin and the laughter of our friends. Help us to notice these special moments and share our gratitude with you, celebrating the joy they bring to our hearts.

HIS MERCY IS NEW TODAY

"The steadfast love of the Lord never ceases; His mercies never come to an end; they are new every morning; great is Your faithfulness." Lamentations 3:22-23

DEVOTIONAL

Every morning is like a fresh start from God. Just as the sun rises each day, His mercy greets us anew. Lamentations 3:22-23 reminds us that God's love is constant and never runs out. No matter what mistakes we make, His forgiveness is waiting for us, ready to help us grow. Today, let's thank God for His loving kindness and remember to share that same love with others. Embrace His mercy, and let it guide your steps!

DAILY REFLECTION

How can you show someone kindness today, reflecting the love and mercy you receive from God?

PRAYER

Dear God, thank you for your endless love and fresh starts every day; help us to remember your mercy and share that kindness with everyone we meet. May our hearts be filled with your grace, guiding our actions as we reflect your love in all that we do.

ROOTED IN GRATITUDE

"Give thanks in all circumstances; for this is the will of God in Christ Jesus for you."
1 Thessalonians 5:18

DEVOTIONAL

In every situation we face, God asks us to give thanks. This means finding good things, even when life is tough. When we practice gratitude, we grow closer to God. We can thank Him for our families, friends, and even the small joys like a sunny day or a favorite snack. Today, take a moment to think of three things you're thankful for. Remember, being grateful helps our hearts, making us stronger in faith and love.

DAILY REFLECTION

As you reflect on your day, take a moment to think about three things that made you smile or brought you joy, even if they were small. How does recognizing these good things help you feel closer to God?

PRAYER

Dear God, thank You for the many blessings in our lives, big and small, that help us smile and feel Your love. Help us to find joy in every moment and to share our gratitude with others, drawing us closer to You each day.

OVERFLOWING WITH THANKSGIVING

"Let your roots grow down into him, and let your lives be built on him. Then your faith will grow strong in the truth you were taught, and you will overflow with thankfulness."
Colossians 2:7

DEVOTIONAL

When we grow our roots deep in Jesus, we begin to understand how much He loves us. As we learn more about Him, our hearts fill with gratitude. Every day, we can thank God for the little things—like a sunny sky or a friend's smile. As our faith grows stronger, our thankfulness overflows, like a cup filled to the brim! Remember, the more we trust Jesus, the more joy and gratitude we can share with others.

DAILY REFLECTION

What is one small thing you can thank God for today that makes you feel joy, and how can you share that thankfulness with someone else?

PRAYER

Dear God, thank you for your love that helps us grow strong like the roots of a tree, filling our hearts with joy and gratitude for the little things around us. Please help us remember to share our thankfulness with others, so they can feel your love too.

GOD'S FAITHFULNESS THROUGH GENERATIONS

"His faithfulness continues through all generations." Psalm 100:5

DEVOTIONAL

God's faithfulness is like a strong bridge connecting generations. In Psalm 100:5, we learn that God is always true to His promises, no matter how many years pass. Just as the sun rises each day, God's love and care are always there for us. When we look back at our families, we can see how God has been with them, just as He is with you today. Trust in His faithfulness, and share His love with others!

DAILY REFLECTION

As you think about God's faithfulness in your life and in your family, how can you share a story of His love or a promise kept with someone close to you?

PRAYER

Dear God, thank you for being a strong bridge that connects us across time with Your unwavering love and promises. Help me to share the stories of Your faithfulness in my life and my family's, so others can feel the warmth of Your care and know they are never alone.

BLESSED TO BE A BLESSING

"Blessed are those who are generous, because they feed the poor." Proverbs 22:9

DEVOTIONAL

Being generous is like sharing sunshine. When we help others, we let God's love shine through us! Proverbs 22:9 reminds us that when we give to those in need, we're spreading joy and kindness. Think about ways you can help today, whether by sharing a toy, lending a hand, or simply being friendly. Each act of kindness makes the world brighter. Remember, when we bless others, we become a blessing in return. Let's warm hearts together!

DAILY REFLECTION

How can you show kindness to someone today, and what small act of generosity can you do to let God's love shine through you?

PRAYER

Dear God, thank you for the gift of kindness and the warmth of your love that shines through us when we help others. Please guide me in finding small ways to share joy today, whether through a smile, a helping hand, or sharing my toys, so that together we can make the world brighter.

FINDING JOY IN SIMPLICITY

"Better is a little with the fear of the Lord than great treasure and trouble therewith." Proverbs 15:16

DEVOTIONAL

In a world that often values big things, like fancy toys and wealth, God reminds us in Proverbs 15:16 that true joy comes from having a heart that loves Him. It's better to have a small gift, a simple meal, or just a few friends who share your faith than to have lots of treasures that bring worry. Let's cherish the little things, like a sunny day or a kind word, and find happiness in being close to God.

DAILY REFLECTION

As you think about the little things that bring you joy in life, what are some simple moments or gifts you can cherish today that help you feel closer to God?

PRAYER

Dear God, thank you for the simple joys in life, like a warm smile from a friend or the beauty of a sunny day, which remind us that true happiness comes from loving you and one another. Help us to cherish these little moments and always find delight in your presence.

GRACE TO END THE MONTH WELL

"Prepare the way for the Lord; make straight paths for him." Mark 1:3

DEVOTIONAL

As we reach the end of the month, remember that God's grace is always with us. In 2 Corinthians 9:8, we learn that God can bless us in every situation. This means we can trust Him to provide everything we need to do good in the world. Take a moment to reflect on your month—what blessings have you received? Let this be a time to celebrate God's goodness and to share His love with others. Embrace His grace and finish strong!

DAILY REFLECTION

As you reflect on your month, think about a time when you felt God's grace in your life. How did that experience inspire you to share love or goodness with others?

PRAYER

Dear God, thank you for your endless grace that surrounds us every day and for the blessings we have received this month. Help us to reflect on your goodness and to share your love with others, so we can shine your light in the world around us.

PREPARING HIM ROOM

"Prepare the way for the Lord; make straight paths for him." Mark 1:3

DEVOTIONAL

As we prepare for Jesus in our lives, think about making space for Him. Just like cleaning your room makes it nice and welcoming, we can clear our hearts. Talk to God, read the Bible, and be kind to others. When we invite Jesus in, He fills us with joy and love. Remember, preparing a path for Him means being open and ready to grow. Each day is a chance to welcome Him more deeply into our hearts.

DAILY REFLECTION

As you think about making space for Jesus in your life, what are some ways you can "clean" your heart and let Him fill you with joy and love? What small actions can you take each day to be more open and inviting to Him?

PRAYER

Dear God, help us to clear our hearts and make space for Jesus, inviting His joy and love into our lives. Guide us in sharing kindness with others and in little actions every day that open the path for Him to grow deeper within us.

PEACE IN THE WAITING

"But those who hope in the Lord will renew their strength. They will soar on wings like eagles; they will run and not grow weary, they will walk and not be faint." Isaiah 40:31

DEVOTIONAL

Waiting can be hard, but it's a special time to grow closer to God. In Isaiah 40:31, we learn that when we put our hopes in Him, He gives us strength. Like eagles soaring high in the sky, we can rise above our worries. While we wait, let's trust that God is working for us. Remember, even if it feels slow, He is with us every step. Take a moment to pray and feel His peace today.

DAILY REFLECTION

As you think about waiting and trusting in God, how can you recognize the moments when He is providing you with strength during challenging times? Write down a situation where you can feel His presence and support while you are waiting.

PRAYER

Dear God, thank you for being with us as we wait, helping us to grow closer to You and find strength in our hopes. Help us to recognize Your presence through our challenges, reminding us that like eagles soaring in the sky, we are never alone.

As for the situation where I can feel Your presence while waiting, I remember a time when I felt nervous about a big test. Even though I was anxious, I sensed Your calmness surrounding me, guiding me to trust in my preparation and in Your support, giving me the courage to face it with confidence.

THE GIFT OF HOPE

"For I know the plans I have for you, declares the Lord, plans to prosper you and not to harm you, plans to give you hope and a future." Jeremiah 29:11

DEVOTIONAL

Hope is a beautiful gift from God! In Jeremiah 29:11, we learn that God has wonderful plans for each of us. These plans are meant to help us grow and thrive. Sometimes, life can be tough, and we may feel scared or lost. But remember, God is always with you, guiding you to a bright future. Trust Him, and hold on to the hope He gives. Each day is a step closer to His amazing plans for your life.

DAILY REFLECTION

How can you remind yourself to trust in God's plans for your life, especially when you feel scared or uncertain?

PRAYER

Dear God, thank you for the beautiful gift of hope that shines bright in my heart, reminding me that you have wonderful plans for my life. Help me to trust in your guidance, especially when I feel scared or lost, and fill me with peace as I step forward each day.

EMMANUEL—GOD WITH US

"For to us a child is born, to us a son is given, and the government will be on his shoulders. And he will be called Wonderful Counselor, Mighty God, Everlasting Father, Prince of Peace." Isaiah 9:6

DEVOTIONAL

In Isaiah 9:6, we learn about Emmanuel, which means "God With Us." God sent His Son, Jesus, to be our friend and helper. Jesus is called the Wonderful Counselor, meaning He gives us wise advice when we feel lost. He is our Mighty God, strong enough to help us through any trouble. When we feel lonely, we can remember that Jesus, our Everlasting Father, is always here, bringing us peace and love every day. Trust Him!

DAILY REFLECTION

Think about a time when you felt alone or needed help. How can remembering that Jesus is always with you as your friend and helper make you feel better in those moments?

PRAYER

Dear Jesus, thank you for being our wonderful friend who is always with us and ready to help when we feel alone or need guidance. Please fill our hearts with your peace and love, reminding us that we are never truly by ourselves and that we can always trust in you.

LETTING GOD INTERRUPT YOUR PLANS

"Many are the plans in a person's heart, but it is the Lord's purpose that prevails."
Proverbs 19:21

DEVOTIONAL

Sometimes, we make plans and daydream about what we want to do. But God has a special purpose for each of us, as Proverbs 19:21 reminds us. It's okay when things don't go as we hoped; that can be God's way of guiding us to something better. When He interrupts our plans, it's a chance to trust Him more. Let's welcome these moments, knowing that God's purpose is always for our good. Keep your heart open to His surprises!

DAILY REFLECTION

Reflect on a time when things didn't go as you had planned. How did that situation turn out differently than you expected, and what did you learn about trusting God during that experience?

PRAYER

Dear God, thank you for the wonderful plans you have for each of us, even when things don't go the way we hoped. Help us to trust you more during those unexpected moments, knowing that your surprises lead us to something beautiful and better than we can imagine.

THE LIGHT HAS COME

"The light shines in the darkness, and the darkness has not overcome it." John 1:5

DEVOTIONAL

In the darkness, we can sometimes feel lost or scared. But remember, Jesus is like a bright light shining in those tough times. John 1:5 tells us that no darkness can put out this light. When we feel sad or alone, we can turn to Him. He brings hope and joy, showing us the way even when things seem difficult. Let's trust in His light every day and share that light with others around us, bringing warmth and love to their hearts.

DAILY REFLECTION

How can you be a light for someone who might be feeling lost or scared today?

PRAYER

Dear Jesus, thank you for being our bright light when things feel dark and scary; please help us trust in your love and share your warmth with others who might be feeling lost. Help us to be a shining light in someone's life today, bringing joy and comfort to their hearts.

HE FULFILLS HIS PROMISES

"God is not man, that he should lie, or a son of man, that he should change his mind; has he said, and will he not do it? Or has he spoken, and will he not fulfill it?" Numbers 23:19

DEVOTIONAL

God always keeps His promises. Unlike people, He never lies or changes His Mind. If God says He will do something, you can be sure that He will. Think about a time when you waited for something great to happen, like a surprise gift or a fun day with friends. Trusting God is like that. He always fulfills His promises because He loves you. Remember to look for those promises each day; they are a sign of His care for you.

DAILY REFLECTION

Think about a time when you had to wait for something exciting, like a special event or a surprise. How did it feel to wait, and what helped you trust that it would happen? Now, consider a promise that God has made to you. How can you remind yourself of that promise in your daily life?

PRAYER

Dear God, thank you for always keeping Your promises and for being someone we can trust completely. Help us remember Your love and faithfulness each day, especially when we're waiting for something wonderful to happen, so we can find joy and hope in Your words.

A SEASON OF SURRENDER

"Trust in the Lord with all your heart and lean not on your own understanding." Proverbs 3:5

DEVOTIONAL

In life, we often think we have all the answers, but God invites us to trust Him wholeheartedly. Proverbs 3:5 reminds us to let go of our own understanding and rely on His wisdom. Surrendering means recognizing that God knows what is best for us, even when we feel confused. This season of surrender brings peace and helps us grow closer to Him. When we trust God fully, we discover His plans are always better than our own.

DAILY REFLECTION

Think about a time when you felt unsure or confused about a situation in your life. How can you practice trusting God more in that area, and what steps can you take to surrender your worries to Him, believing that His plans are better than your own?

PRAYER

Dear God, help us to remember that even when we feel confused, we can trust in Your wisdom and love. Teach us to surrender our worries to You, believing that Your plans for our lives are always better than our own.

WELCOMING WONDER

"Behold, I am doing a new thing; now it springs forth, do you not perceive it?" Isaiah 43:19

DEVOTIONAL

God loves to surprise us with His plans! In Isaiah 43:19, He tells us, "Behold, I am doing a new thing." This means we should open our hearts to new experiences and blessings God has for us. Each day can bring fresh ideas, friendships, and joy. Instead of looking for the same routine, let's notice the wonderful surprises around us. Trust that God is always at work, ready to lead us on exciting paths of faith and discovery.

DAILY REFLECTION

What is one new experience or blessing you can look for this week that you believe God might be showing you? How can you open your heart to receive it?

PRAYER

Dear God, thank you for the wonderful surprises you have in store for us every day. Help us to open our hearts to the new experiences and blessings you want to share, so we can trust in your amazing plans for our lives.

TRUSTING THROUGH TRANSITION

"Trust in the Lord with all your heart and lean not on your own understanding." Proverbs 3:5

DEVOTIONAL

When life changes, it can be hard to know what to do. But remember Proverbs 3:5: "Trust in the Lord with all your heart." This means we should rely on God, not just on what we think. When you face a new school, move to a different place, or feel nervous about something, talk to God. He loves you and will guide you through any transition. Trust Him fully, and you will find peace and strength.

DAILY REFLECTION

Think about a time when you faced a big change in your life, like starting at a new school or moving to a new place. How did you feel during that transition? Write down a prayer asking God for help and guidance, trusting that He will give you the peace and strength you need. What is one specific thing you can do this week to remind yourself to trust in Him during changes?

PRAYER

Dear God, when changes feel overwhelming and I'm unsure of what to do, please help me to trust in You with my whole heart, knowing that You are always by my side. Let me feel Your love guiding me through each new experience, bringing me peace and strength as I navigate these transitions.

December 11

THE STRENGTH OF A WILLING HEART

"For I can do everything through Christ, who gives me strength."
Philippians 4:13

DEVOTIONAL

In our journey of faith, having a willing heart is powerful. Philippians 4:13 reminds us that we can do everything through Christ, who strengthens us. When we face challenges, we might feel scared or weak, but with a heart ready to trust and follow God, we can overcome anything. Remember, it's not about being the strongest but being willing to let God help you. Each day, open your heart and see how God empowers you to grow and shine.

DAILY REFLECTION

Take a moment to think about a challenge you're currently facing. How can you open your heart to God in this situation, and what does it mean for you to trust that He will strengthen you to overcome it? Consider sharing your thoughts with someone, or jot them down in a journal.

PRAYER

Dear God, help me to open my heart to You, trusting that You will give me the strength to face my challenges. Remind me that with Your love and guidance, I can overcome anything that comes my way.

December 12

HEAVEN'S PERSPECTIVE

"Set your minds on things that are above, not on things that are on earth." Colossians 3:2

DEVOTIONAL

Heaven's perspective invites us to look beyond our daily worries and troubles. In Colossians 3:2, we are reminded to focus on the wonderful things God has in store for us. When we think about heaven, we remember that God loves us deeply and has a perfect plan for our future. Each day, let's choose to love others, share kindness, and grow in our faith. By setting our minds on heavenly things, we find peace and joy in our hearts.

DAILY REFLECTION

How can remembering the good things God has for you help you handle your worries today? Think about a way you can show kindness to someone or share love with others this week.

PRAYER

Dear God, thank you for the beautiful gifts you have in store for us and for reminding us to focus on your love and plans for our lives. Help us to share kindness and joy with those around us, so we can reflect your love and find peace in our hearts amid any worries we face.

FINDING JOY IN CHRIST

"Rejoice in the Lord always; again I will say, rejoice!" Philippians 4:4

DEVOTIONAL

Finding joy in Christ means looking for happiness in Him every day. Philippians 4:4 reminds us to "rejoice in the Lord always." This means we can celebrate God's love no matter what happens. When we focus on His goodness, we see His blessings, even in tough times. Try to thank God for little things, like a beautiful day or a kind friend. As you do, you'll feel joy grow in your heart, bringing you closer to Him.

DAILY REFLECTION

Think about a recent moment when you felt happy or grateful. How did that moment help you see God's goodness in your life? What small blessings can you thank Him for today?

PRAYER

Dear God, thank you for filling our hearts with joy and love, reminding us to celebrate your goodness every day. Help us to notice and appreciate the little blessings in our lives, and may each moment of gratitude bring us closer to You.

HOLDING SPACE FOR SILENCE

"Be still, and know that I am God." Psalm 46:10

DEVOTIONAL

Take a moment to stop and be quiet. The Bible reminds us in Psalm 46:10 to "Be still, and know that I am God." In the hustle and bustle of life, it's easy to forget to listen. God wants to speak to you in those quiet moments. When you find space for silence, you can feel His presence and hear His voice more clearly. Try sitting in stillness today; it's a wonderful way to connect with Him.

DAILY REFLECTION

Take a moment to think about a time when you felt really calm and still. How did that quietness help you feel closer to God? What can you do today to create a little space for silence and to listen for His voice?

PRAYER

Dear God, thank You for the special moments of quiet where we can feel Your love and hear Your voice. Help us to find time in our busy days to be still, so we can grow closer to You and listen to the whispers of Your heart.

RECEIVING GOD'S PEACE

"Peace I leave with you; my peace I give you." John 14:27

DEVOTIONAL

In John 14:27, Jesus offers us a wonderful gift: His peace. When we're feeling worried or afraid, we can remember that Jesus is with us. His peace is different from what the world gives; it's calm and strong. To receive His peace, we can take a moment to pray, asking Him to fill our hearts. Let's trust that Jesus wants us to feel safe and loved. Each day, let His peace guide your thoughts and actions.

DAILY REFLECTION

How can you remind yourself of Jesus' peace when you're feeling worried or afraid, and what steps can you take to invite that peace into your daily life?

PRAYER

Dear Jesus, thank you for your beautiful gift of peace that helps us feel safe and loved even when we are worried or afraid. Please fill my heart with your calm and strong peace, guiding my thoughts and actions each day as I trust in your presence.

AN INVITATION TO STILLNESS

"Be still, and know that I am God." Psalm 46:10

DEVOTIONAL

In our busy lives, it's easy to forget to pause and listen. Psalm 46:10 reminds us, "Be still, and know that I am God." God invites us to find moments of quiet, where we can feel His presence and love. When we stop to be still, we open our hearts to hear His voice and understand His plans for us. This week, try to take a few minutes each day to breathe deeply, pray, and simply be with God.

DAILY REFLECTION

Take a moment to think about your day. Can you find a few quiet minutes to just sit, breathe, and listen for God's voice? What might you feel or hear when you take that time to be still with Him?

PRAYER

Dear God, thank you for inviting us to be still and feel your love in our busy lives. Help us find quiet moments each day to listen for your voice and discover your beautiful plans for us.

Near the End of Our Journey

You have spent many days reflecting through these devotionals.

If this book has supported your spiritual journey, sharing a short review on Amazon helps more women discover these pages of encouragement.

devo.anchoredgraces.com/workingmoms

Your story may be the reason another woman finds hope.

THE HEART OF GENEROSITY

"Each of you should give what you have decided in your heart to give, not reluctantly or under compulsion, for God loves a cheerful giver." 2 Corinthians 9:7

DEVOTIONAL

Generosity starts in our hearts. God wants us to share our gifts and blessings joyfully, not because we have to, but because we want to. When we give with a cheerful heart, we show love to others and to God. Think about what you can share today—time, toys, or a kind word. Remember, it's not about how much you give, but the love behind it. Let's practice generosity and watch how it brings us closer to God!

DAILY REFLECTION

What is one special thing you can share with someone today that will brighten their day and show them you care? Think about how it might feel to give that gift from your heart.

PRAYER

Dear God, thank you for the blessings You have given us and the joy we feel when we share from our hearts. Help us to find one special way to show our love to others today, knowing that every kind gesture brings us closer to You.

GOD'S PERFECT TIMING

"To everything there is a season, a time for every purpose under heaven." Ecclesiastes 3:1

DEVOTIONAL

God has a perfect plan for each of us, and part of that plan includes timing. Ecclesiastes 3:1 tells us there is a season for everything. Sometimes we may want things to happen right away, but God knows the best time for us. When we trust Him and wait patiently, we can find peace in knowing He is working behind the scenes. Let's remember to pray and trust that God's timing is always perfect, even when we can't see it.

DAILY REFLECTION

Think about a time when you wanted something to happen quickly, but it didn't go the way you expected. How did you feel during that waiting period? Reflect on how trusting in God's timing might change your perspective when you find yourself waiting again. What steps can you take to find peace in that waiting?

PRAYER

Dear God, thank you for having a special plan for each of us, reminding us that everything happens in its own perfect time. Help us to trust you during our waiting, finding peace in the moments of uncertainty, and believing that you are always working things out for our good.

RESTING IN HIS GOODNESS

"Come to me, all you who are weary and burdened, and I will give you rest." Matthew 11:28

DEVOTIONAL

When you feel tired or worried, remember Jesus invites you to come to Him. In Matthew 11:28, He promises to give rest to those who are weary. Just like a warm hug comforts you, spending time with God brings peace. Find a quiet place, talk to Him, and share your feelings. Trust that He cares for you and wants to lift your burdens. Rest in His goodness, knowing He is always there to help and comfort you.

DAILY REFLECTION

Think about a time when you felt tired or worried. How can you take a moment now to share those feelings with Jesus, and what do you think it means to rest in His goodness?

PRAYER

Dear Jesus, when I feel tired or worried, I come to you just like you invited me to. Please help me to share my feelings with you and to rest in your goodness, knowing you are always here to lift me up and bring me peace.

HE CAME FOR YOU

"For God so loved the world that he gave his one and only Son, that whoever believes in him shall not perish but have eternal life." John 3:16

DEVOTIONAL

God loves each of us so much that He gave us a wonderful gift—His Son, Jesus. This gift means we can have a special friendship with God, not just today but forever! When we believe in Jesus, we discover that we are never alone; He is always with us. Take a moment each day to talk to God, read the Bible, and feel His love. Remember, Jesus came just for you, and He wants to help you grow in faith!

DAILY REFLECTION

How can you take a moment today to talk to God and feel His love, knowing that Jesus is always with you as your special friend?

PRAYER

Dear God, thank you for the amazing gift of Jesus, who shows us how much You love us and invites us to be Your special friends. Help me take a moment each day to talk to You, feel Your love, and remember that with Jesus by my side, I am never alone.

AWE AND ADORATION

"Great is the Lord, and greatly to be praised; his greatness is unsearchable." Psalm 145:3

DEVOTIONAL

God is truly amazing! Psalm 145:3 reminds us that our Lord is great and deserves all our praise. Every day, we can find something wonderful about Him—like the beauty of creation or the joy of friendship. When we take time to admire God's greatness, our hearts fill with awe and love. Let's spend a moment today remembering all the good things He has done. Praise Him for who He is, and let your heart sing with joy!

DAILY REFLECTION

Think about a moment this week when you felt joy or saw something beautiful in nature. How can you connect that feeling to how amazing God is? Take a moment to praise Him for that experience and how it shows His greatness.

PRAYER

Dear God, thank you for the amazing beauty in the world around us and the joy we feel in our hearts. Help us to see all the wonderful things you have created and to always remember to praise you for your greatness.

GRACE FOR THE HOLIDAYS

"But he said to me, 'My grace is sufficient for you, for my power is made perfect in weakness.'" 2 Corinthians 12:9

DEVOTIONAL

As we celebrate the holidays, remember that God's grace is a wonderful gift! In 2 Corinthians 12:9, God reminds us that His grace is enough for every challenge we face. During this busy season, it's okay to feel overwhelmed or weak. Instead of relying on our strength, we can trust that God's power shines brightest in our moments of struggle. Let's embrace His grace, share love with others, and find joy in His presence.

DAILY REFLECTION

As you think about the challenges you faced this year, how can you see God's grace at work in those moments, and how might you share that grace and love with someone else during the holidays?

PRAYER

Dear God, thank you for your amazing grace that helps us through tough times and fills our hearts with love. Please help us to share that grace with others this holiday season, reminding them of your kindness and bringing joy to those around us.

WRAPPED IN HIS LOVE

"For I am convinced that neither death nor life, neither angels nor demons, neither the present nor the future, nor any powers, will be able to separate us from the love of God that is in Christ Jesus our Lord." Romans 8:38-39

DEVOTIONAL

In life, we experience many ups and downs, but God's love is always there, wrapping around us like a warm blanket. Romans 8:38-39 reminds us that nothing can take us away from His love—neither good days nor bad. When you feel scared or alone, remember that Jesus is with you. Take a moment to pray and feel His love surrounding you. Each day is a chance to grow closer to Him and share that love with others.

DAILY REFLECTION

Reflect on a time when you felt scared or alone. How can you remember that God's love is with you in those moments? Take a moment to think about how you can share that love with someone else today. What is one kind thing you could do for someone who might also be feeling down?

PRAYER

Dear God, thank You for always being with us, wrapping us in Your love during our happy and tough times. Help us to remember Your presence when we feel scared or alone, and guide us to share that warmth with others who need it.

A HOLY NIGHT

"For unto us a child is born, unto us a son is given." Isaiah 9:6

DEVOTIONAL

On that holy night, a special gift came to us: Jesus, the Son of God! Isaiah 9:6 reminds us that this child brings hope, love, and light into our lives. When we celebrate His birth, we remember that He came just for us. Each time we feel lonely or scared, we can look to Jesus for comfort and guidance. Let's share His love with others, just like He shared His heart with us on that beautiful night.

DAILY REFLECTION

What is one way you can share love and kindness with someone today, just as Jesus shared His love with us on that special night?

PRAYER

Dear God, thank You for the precious gift of Jesus, who brings us hope, love, and light. Help us to share that same love with others, so they can feel Your kindness shining through us today.

December 25

JOY TO THE WORLD

"Shout for joy to the Lord, all the earth." Psalm 100:1

DEVOTIONAL

Joy to the world means sharing happiness with everyone! Psalm 100:1 reminds us to shout for joy, praising God for His love. Imagine how the earth sings with joy when we smile, help others, and share kind words. Each day is a special gift from God, and we can celebrate it by loving Him and those around us. Let's spread joy like confetti, knowing that our happy hearts can brighten the world and draw us closer to God.

DAILY REFLECTION

How can you share joy with someone today, and what kind words or actions will you use to make their day a little brighter?

PRAYER

Dear God, thank you for the gift of joy that comes from sharing love and kindness with others. Help us to spread happiness like confetti today, bringing smiles and warm hearts to everyone we meet.

December 26

PEACE BEYOND THE PRESENTS

"And the peace of God, which surpasses all understanding, will guard your hearts and minds through Christ Jesus." Philippians 4:7

DEVOTIONAL

Amidst the excitement of gifts and celebrations, remember that true peace comes from God. The Bible tells us in Philippians 4:7 that His peace is greater than anything we can understand. While presents can bring joy, they can't fill our hearts like God can. Take a moment to pray and invite His peace into your life. Trust that He is always with you, guarding your heart and helping you feel calm, even in busy times.

DAILY REFLECTION

How can you invite God's peace into your heart today, especially when the joy from gifts and celebrations starts to feel overwhelming?

PRAYER

Dear God, thank you for all the joy that gifts and celebrations bring, but help us remember that your peace is even greater and can fill our hearts in the busiest moments. Please calm our minds and remind us that you are always with us, guiding us to feel your love and tranquility in every situation.

LOOKING BACK WITH GRATITUDE

"Give thanks to the Lord, for he is good; his love endures forever." 1 Chronicles 16:34

DEVOTIONAL

As we look back on our days, let's remember all the good things God has done for us. Take a moment to think about your family, friends, and even the little joys, like a sunny day or a favorite snack. Each blessing reminds us of God's love, which is always there. In 1 Chronicles 16:34, we're encouraged to give thanks. Let's make gratitude a habit, knowing that God's goodness never fades and His love is forever strong.

DAILY REFLECTION

What is one thing you are thankful for today that reminds you of God's love? How does that make you feel?

PRAYER

Dear God, thank you for all the wonderful things in our lives, from family and friends to sunny days and yummy snacks. Help us to remember your love in every blessing we receive and to always feel grateful in our hearts.

PREPARING FOR THE NEW

"Behold, I am doing a new thing; now it springs forth, do you not perceive it?" Isaiah 43:19

DEVOTIONAL

God is always at work, bringing new things into our lives. In Isaiah 43:19, He tells us He is doing something amazing! To prepare for the new, we can pray and ask God to open our eyes to see His plans. Look for opportunities to love others and grow in kindness. Remember, change can be exciting and scary, but with God's help, we can embrace what He has for us. Let's trust Him as we step into the new!

DAILY REFLECTION

What are some new things you see happening in your life, and how can you pray and act to show love and kindness as you embrace these changes?

PRAYER

Dear God, thank you for always working in our lives and for the amazing new things you bring our way. Help us to see your plans with open hearts and to share love and kindness with others as we embrace the changes ahead.

HE'S ALREADY IN TOMORROW

"For I know the plans I have for you, declares the Lord, plans to prosper you and not to harm you, plans to give you hope and a future." Jeremiah 29:11

DEVOTIONAL

When we wake up each day, it's easy to worry about what tomorrow will bring. But remember, God has great plans for you! Jeremiah 29:11 reminds us that He knows the future and wants to give you hope. He's already in tomorrow, preparing good things for you. Instead of being afraid, trust in His plan. Pray each day, asking Him to guide you. With God, you can face anything, knowing He is with you every step of the way.

DAILY REFLECTION

What are some things you can do to put your trust in God each day, knowing He has good plans for you?

PRAYER

Dear God, thank You for always being with us and for the wonderful plans You have in store. Help us to trust in Your goodness every day, knowing that You are preparing a bright future filled with hope and joy.

FINISHING THE YEAR IN FAITH

"Let us run with perseverance the race marked out for us, fixing our eyes on Jesus." Hebrews 12:1-2

DEVOTIONAL

As we approach the end of the year, let's remember to run our race with faith! Just like a runner focuses on the finish line, we can fix our eyes on Jesus. He gives us strength and courage to keep going, even when times are tough. Take a moment each day to pray and read the Bible. Let God guide you and help you grow in love and kindness as you prepare for the new year ahead.

DAILY REFLECTION

As you think about running your race with faith, what is one thing you can do each day to focus on Jesus and grow in love and kindness as you get ready for the new year?

PRAYER

Dear God, as we run our race with faith, help us to keep our eyes on Jesus and find strength in His love. May we discover small ways each day to show kindness and grow in Your love as we prepare for the new year ahead.

GOD'S FAITHFULNESS NEVER ENDS

"The steadfast love of the Lord never ceases; his mercies never come to an end." Lamentations 3:22

DEVOTIONAL

God's love for you is like a warm, cozy blanket that never wears out. In Lamentations 3:22, we learn that God's kindness always stays the same and never goes away. No matter how tough life gets or how many mistakes we make, God is always there, ready to help us start fresh. Each day is a chance to feel His love and to share that love with others. Remember, God's faithfulness is with you all the time!

DAILY REFLECTION

Reflect on a time when you felt loved and cared for by someone. How did it make you feel? Now, think about how God's love is always there for you, just like that warm, cozy blanket. How can you share that feeling of love with someone else today?

PRAYER

Dear God, thank you for Your love that wraps around us like a warm, cozy blanket, always keeping us safe and comforted. Help us to share Your kindness with others so they can feel Your warmth and care just like we do.

More Devotionals from Anchored Grace

If this devotional encouraged your heart, you may also enjoy these devotionals from Anchored Grace.

- 365 Day Devotional for Women
- 90 Day Devotional for Women Seeking Peace
- 90 Day Devotional for Women Facing Anxiety and Stress
- 90 Day Devotional for Women 50+
- Guided Prayer Journal for Women

Search **"Anchored Grace Devotional"** on Amazon to discover more devotionals designed to support your journey of faith.

Thank You
for Walking This Journey

Thank you for spending this devotional journey with Anchored Grace.

If this devotional encouraged your heart, strengthened your faith, or brought peace to your daily routine, would you consider leaving a short review on Amazon?

devo.anchoredgraces.com/workingmoms

Reviews help other women discover devotionals that may support them through their own seasons of life.

Even a single sentence about your experience can make a difference.

We are grateful you chose Anchored Grace.